PLAN, NOT PANIC

IT'S TIME TO
PLAN, NOT PANIC

Emergency Evacuation Preparedness and Coping Skills

Barbara Salsbury

ISBN 13: 978-0-88290-810-3
ISBN 10: 0-88290-810-3

Published by Horizon, an imprint of Cedar Fort, Inc.
925 N. Main, Springville, UT, 84663
Distributed by Cedar Fort, Inc. www.cedarfort.com

Cover design by Nicole Williams
Cover design © 2006 by Lyle Mortimer
Printed in the United States of America

10 9 8 7 6 5 4 3 2 1

Printed on acid-free paper

CONTENTS

CHAPTER ONE

IT'S TIME TO PLAN, NOT PANIC

Are you answering the wake-up call, or have you shut off the alarm? Wake-up calls have gone out to most of the world. They came at the terrifying Richter-scale readings of 9.0 and 8.0, and with category 5 hurricane wind-speeds of 145–75 mph. They sounded during hurricanes Katrina, Rita, and Wilma, to mention a few. Are you answering the call, or shutting off the alarm and "snoozing" for a while longer? The wake-up calls referred to are, of course, the continuing series of natural and man-made disasters that afflict the nation and the world.

As the anguish of others going through these disasters fades from the headlines and the nightly news, our resolve to do something about our own situation fades along with the reports. We quickly slip back into everyday living, lulled by the hope that if we don't think about a potential disaster it will never happen to us. After all, disasters only happen to somebody else, right?

Disaster! Crisis! Emergency! These words may give you feelings of apathy or terror, depending on whether or not you have experienced the things the words describe. Most disasters are sudden and unexpected, and many people are unprepared for the problems a disaster may bring. After all, how many of your neighbors do you know who know which day their disaster is coming? Most of you have been exposed to countless disasters. There are newspaper accounts of train wrecks, plane crashes, house fires, hurricanes, tornadoes, and chemical spills, and reports of them are presented on television in living color. Hollywood has produced dozens of disaster films that leave their viewers with the perception that disasters are what happen to somebody else.

We say, "My hair is a disaster!" or "The kitchen is a disaster!" or "The vacation was an absolute disaster!"—expressions that reduce the value of life-threatening and life-altering disasters to simple pocket change.

Sooner or later, you may be forced to leave your home, even if only temporarily, because of some kind of emergency. Earthquakes, tornadoes, wildfires, floods, and

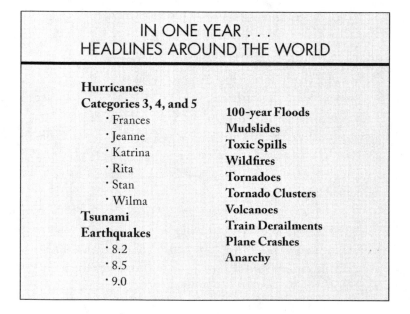

IN ONE YEAR . . .
HEADLINES AROUND THE WORLD

Hurricanes
Categories 3, 4, and 5
- Frances
- Jeanne
- Katrina
- Rita
- Stan
- Wilma

Tsunami
Earthquakes
- 8.2
- 8.5
- 9.0

100-year Floods
Mudslides
Toxic Spills
Wildfires
Tornadoes
Tornado Clusters
Volcanoes
Train Derailments
Plane Crashes
Anarchy

hurricanes can occur almost anywhere and at any time, sometimes at the same time.

To the natural disasters we can add a long list of man-made problems such as explosions, leakage of hazardous chemicals or radioactive waste. Then there is terrorism—so difficult to even comprehend but which can suddenly affect thousands of lives and create the necessity of rapid evacuation.

Let me share a page from my personal journal dated October 17, 1989, written in Santa Clara, California. "At 5:04 tonight I was sitting at my desk putting the final touches on a presentation to an Emergency Preparedness committee. I felt a strong jolt, and then literally all heck broke loose. I raced for the bathroom doorway. I had to force myself to try to think so I could figure out what to do next. Within thirty seconds there was no heat, light, power, water, phones, or security. At least I'm alive. The reports on the radio are becoming more and more graphic as the aftershocks continue their unrelenting battering. As night and darkness descend, it's apparent that the suffering is escalating at an overwhelming rate."

DALLIN H. OAKS ON NATURAL DISASTERS

[Natural disasters] are all around us and seem to be increasing in frequency and intensity. For example, the list of major earthquakes in *The World Almanac and Book of Facts, 2004* shows twice as many earthquakes in the decades of the 1980s and 1990s as in the two preceding decades 1988–90). It also shows further sharp increases in the first several years of this century. The list of notable floods and tidal waves and the list of hurricanes, typhoons, and blizzards worldwide show similar increases in recent years. Increases by comparison with 50 years ago can be dismissed as changes in reporting criteria, but the accelerating pattern of natural disasters in the last few decades is ominous. ("Preparation for the Second Coming," *Ensign*, May 2004, 8)

A few other recent disasters are still fresh in our memories. Who can forget the deadly tsunami in Indonesia that affected so many countries? Who could ever have imagined four deadly hurricanes hitting one state within such a short time? Katrina and Wilma are not the names of relatives we'd want to claim, since they arrived with such destruction. They also created evacuation lines that caused hours of fear for people caught in giant gridlock on the freeways. In the last few years it hasn't always been somebody *else* that *it* happened to. There have been so many people displaced, so many people out of homes!

The Significance of Personal Preparation

Disasters are increasing, not decreasing throughout the world. When disaster strikes, people invariably are forced to flee from their homes. Perhaps not everyone will have to do this. Shouldn't you be prepared so that if you have to leave your home, even if only for a few hours, you can do so with a minimum of discomfort? The fact is your preparation may even save your life or the lives of your family.

Still, many people are apathetic about preparing for disaster. Often it is because they just don't know what to do. People are simply so overwhelmed at the prospect that they become discouraged before they begin. Others run to and fro gathering information—that can be frustrating because it seems to be contradictory. Yet other information is so blatantly commercial, tied to outlets or products, that people tend to doubt the validity of it. Others do nothing, figuring that if trouble comes, an emergency disaster organization will rush to their rescue. Thousands of hungry, angry people during the aftermath of Hurricane Katrina in New Orleans in 2005 furiously demanded to know why no help was forthcoming. "Where's the government when you need them?" was a standard outcry.

A common misconception that *must* be refuted is that the government will *immediately* come to your rescue. If you think that the Red Cross or Salvation Army will come running *immediately* to your *individual* rescue, think again. Such agencies do help, but they have to rely heavily on volunteer labor and donated commodities. In a crisis, their immediate efforts must be concentrated on coordinating the greatest amount of relief to the most people as quickly as possible. In a disaster, that may mean bringing in volunteers and organizations from outside

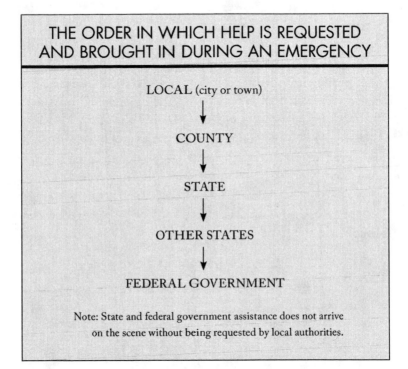

THE ORDER IN WHICH HELP IS REQUESTED AND BROUGHT IN DURING AN EMERGENCY

LOCAL (city or town)

↓

COUNTY

↓

STATE

↓

OTHER STATES

↓

FEDERAL GOVERNMENT

Note: State and federal government assistance does not arrive on the scene without being requested by local authorities.

the disaster area, and that takes time! This does not demean the marvelous service that these organizations perform. It focuses on how immense their responsibilities are and to what degree the public has come to rely solely upon them. It is virtually impossible for such organizations to provide for everyone's

Personal emergency preparedness is everyone's responsibility.

specific individual needs, especially in the first hours of the disaster.

As for your government officials and services, there is a critical concept for individuals and families to understand. City or county personnel usually will be unable to meet the personal needs of individuals; they must first attend to city-wide needs: restoring power, clearing obstructed thoroughfares, setting up and coordinating emergency hospitals, reconnecting communications; therefore, personal emergency preparedness is everyone's responsibility.

As Hurricane Rita rushed toward landfall, miles of cars evacuating Houston, Texas, were shown on the nightly news. Millions trying to escape fled with only the clothes on their backs and the family pet. A few had some supplies; the majority did not. Cars ran out of gas and clogged traffic. It did not take long for the photographers and news camera crews to zoom in on the cars stranded by the side of the freeway with signs propped up that read "We need food," or "We need water." There's a lesson to be learned here.

The Categories of Preparedness

Emergency preparedness can be divided into two basic categories: (1) in the home, and (2) out of the home. The first category—in the home—includes man-made or natural disasters such as severe or violent storms, power outages, floods, riots, and so on. In such instances, normal living may be interrupted for several days or weeks. Your home, if not critically damaged and still deemed safe, could function as a viable shelter even though you could be without utilities. Emergency foods, supplies, and equipment such as fluorescent lanterns or butane stoves and appropriate camping equipment, would enable you to survive the discomfort of such a crisis with relative security.

In some instances, there may be structural or other problems that would necessitate living in the yard in a tent or makeshift shelter, while using your home as a base of supplies and security. A prime example of this situation is the aftermath of a major earthquake. If your home is still standing, there may be the fear, danger, and insecurity of remaining inside until the major aftershocks cease.

The second category—out of the home—include the crises that force you to evacuate from your home and immediate area. In most instances, evacuation is not a matter of choice. It is

---

LAG TIME: AN EXAMPLE

The officers and out-of-state government officials who arrived in Florida to help with the rescue and restoration efforts following several of the devastating hurricanes in the fall of 2005 said over and over again that the crisis and evacuation time frame for restoring normal services would be much longer than 72 hours. In many instances it was weeks before services were restored. In the meantime, tent cities sprang up to attempt to house evacuees, and it was not fun!

---

a life-threatening situation. Once you have been evacuated you most likely will not be allowed to cross back through the police lines until the evacuated area has been declared safe by the authorities. It could last a few hours, days, or weeks. Evacuation-preparedness 72-hour survival supplies and foods need to be considerably different from those that are normally thought of in connection with emergency preparedness. *All food, supplies, equipment, and other essential elements must be portable, packed in small manageable containers and prepared prior to the need.*

Lag Time: A Critical Factor

The "villain" of disasters and emergencies severe enough to cause evacuation is lag time. This is the period between the actual occurrence of the emergency and when organized help arrives. Most people evacuated from their homes do not expect to be away for more than one day. This is a serious misconception. Many evacuation periods last several days or more. For the first hours or even days of an emergency, you alone may have to provide your own food, clothing, and other supplies until help arrives.

Research has shown that in most serious situations, the lag time is *at least* 72 hours: three 24-hour days. During that time, evacuees could be faced with living in fairly primitive conditions. There may not be any clean water, heat, lights, toilet facilities, or shelter. The longer the lag time, the more the problems compound.

While discussing this situation with me, the director of one Utah chapter of the Red Cross commented, "Lag time is not given the emphasis that it should be given. It is one of the most critical factors during an evacuation, yet most people don't even recognize it, let alone prepare for it."

Remember, the disaster has to take place first. Then lag time begins. The call must be placed from the city or town to the Red Cross to put shelters in place. Orders have to be issued and states of emergency declared. If the disaster is a major storm, there may be more units in place and ready to move in, which could shorten the response time, but in such situations, there typically are hundreds of thousands of people needing help.

After the 7.2 Loma Prieta earthquake, I recorded these thoughts: "In a city of hundreds of thousands, the feeling of helplessness and being alone descended immediately. I did not comprehend the extent of the devastation because there were no communications. The battery-powered radio confirmed my worst suspicions. Over and over the broadcasters intoned, 'you will need to take care of yourself for the next several days.'"

Preparation for lag time is a must! Most evacuees have not prepared at all. They simply lock their doors behind them and leave. They survive the displacement, but they enjoy little dignity or comfort during the experience. When people have prepared in advance for evacuation, they have far fewer problems than they would have had. They are somewhat comfortable, have activities to occupy their time, are less concerned about unfinished business, and are less likely to have problems at a shelter.

Analyze the Risks

Analyze the risks in your area. Assess your neighborhood so that you can plan, not panic. As you become aware of the problems that could occur in your neighborhood, the chance that you could be forced to evacuate your home will most likely be brought sharply into focus. When you combine these problems with the possibility of natural disasters, your understanding of the need to prepare an individual evacuation plan and kit becomes even more pronounced. The more detailed your research, the better prepared you will be. Go out into your neighborhood to see what is there. One suggestion is to make your evaluation a family activity, or get together with a neighbor or roommate to survey the situation. If you belong to a neighborhood association, plot the area on a map, accept assignments to divide up the territory, do the research, and share the information. Memory may not be reliable; changes occur constantly. Familiarity allows you to gaze at a scene without recognizing the details of what you are looking at. Look at businesses, such as the common gas station or paint store, with a different perspective. Keep in mind this is planning, not panic. It is simply having the foresight to assess a potential problem and deal with it! As you recognize the existence of the situation or facilities in your area, make note of the specific problems that could arise.

Five-Mile Rule

The area that can directly affect you is usually within a five-mile radius of your home. Of course, Mother Nature cannot be confined to any specific area; she may not abide the five-mile rule. Determine the proximity of freeways, railroads, and factories to your home. What kinds of factories are there? What kind of freight is shipped near you? Think of the specific problems these could cause. For example, are you aware that toxic materials are often transported by truck? If a spill or leak occurs on a nearby highway, you could be evacuated. Railroads also carry substances that could be threatening. Are there tracks near you? Would the nearby geographical terrain ease or aggravate possible problems? Are you in the flood path if a dam or levy should break? Once you have evaluated the surrounding area, you should be able to analyze the perils that would have the greatest effect on you.

Preparations Must Include Practice

As you develop all of the facets of a sound emergency evacuation plan, build practice into it. The drills at home could prove to be priceless if and when the real thing occurs. The main reason for planning, studying, and practicing is that you are more likely to keep your head about you. Practice sessions should focus on those emergencies most likely to occur in your area.

Locate Your Evacuation Shelter

An essential part of practical preparation should be to contact relatives and friends who might live nearby, yet away from your immediate area. Make arrangements to stay with them in case your home might be rendered uninhabitable for several weeks or longer. If staying with a friend or relative is not a possibility, then your option most likely will be a community evacuation shelter. Preparing to survive in the wilderness is not necessary. You will not have to eat weeds or hunt for wild game. In fact, in most areas there aren't even hills to head for. In most areas, schools, churches, National Guard armories, and other large public buildings with large recreation rooms and kitchen facilities are used to house evacuees. An earthquake or major disaster could cause a possible exception, where buildings that would normally be used in your immediate neighborhood to shelter disaster victims would be considered unsafe. Evacuees would then need to stay in tents or makeshift shelters outside. In these instances, as soon as it is possible, the National Guard generally sets up large community tents for public use, and other shelters are opened in neighborhoods close by.

After an emergency occurs, a designated person at the city's Emergency Operations Center calls the Red Cross. The Red Cross then determines where the service center or shelter will be set up. For example, a toxic leak from a train car on a railroad spur forced a neighborhood evacuation in Salt Lake City, Utah, in 2005. The Red Cross was called, and before too long, service centers were set up in two churches outside the evacuation area.

Plan your escape routes on paper now. Assess other neighboring areas to see what churches, armories, schools, fraternal lodges, and other buildings with large recreation rooms and kitchen facilities might be used as evacuation shelters for your area. To determine what buildings are designated as evacuation centers, call your local emergency services office, sheriff's department, police department, or Red Cross director.

In order to eliminate guesswork and confusion at the time of evacuation, buy or draw a large map of your area. Using the results and information from your neighborhood evaluation, mark the routes to several of the buildings you or emergency services have determined to be the most logical evacuation centers. Be sure to record street address numbers. A few practice runs now are essential to creating calm when a crisis comes. At all times, keep this map with your 72-hour evacuation kit.

Answer the Wake-up Call, Accept the Challenge

The clock is ticking; the alarm has already rung. Who knows what time an emergency will keep its appointment with you? Your day planner or palm pilot won't help you now. Don't be caught unprepared! By acting now to be ready for a 72-hour evacuation and existence in a shelter or evacuation area, you will not just survive—you'll survive with dignity, confidence, and even some comfort. Use the following chapters as an outline to determine your individual or family needs. This is not a hard-and-fast, rigid program. It can be adapted to each individual or family in all their different situations. It takes time, effort, planning, and some money, and it usually is not completed overnight. Start now. In a crisis, any preparation, even a minimal kit, would be far superior to having nothing to rely on. Remember: crises and disasters do *not* make appointments before they come calling.

And for those who might be skeptical and ask, "What if I go to all of the effort to create an emergency kit and nothing ever happens?" Call it a security blanket in a box. Be ever so grateful if you never have to use it. However, it only takes once.

CHAPTER TWO

CREATE A KIT

The first and most important thing to do in preparing for an evacuation is to assemble a 72-hour emergency kit for each member of your family. The emergency kits should contain basically what you will need to survive for seventy-two hours or more, including food, clothing, and everything else. These kits must be ready and accessible *before* an evacuation order comes, and how well you prepare them will determine how well you survive a crisis while maintaining some degree of dignity and confidence. If you are forced to evacuate, your kit becomes your "mini-home away from home." Your goal: security—not luxury—in a kit.

All Kits Are Not Created Equal

The ideal portable evacuation kit, in many people's opinion, has four to six wheels attached. It is commonly called a fully equipped motor home, fifth-wheel trailer, or a camper rather than a 72-hour kit. This would indeed be the ultimate solution, meeting all the requirements for an evacuation situation. Of course, if you have to walk out, it would be a bit heavy to carry. Should you own one, keep it stocked with evacuation preparedness in mind. But most of us have to create a kit.

Limited Space: A Key Factor

One of the major differences that sets evacuation preparedness apart from other preparedness categories is the extreme limitation of space. In order to assemble your kit, you must choose a container. All subsequent decisions will be based on the kind and size of container you choose. All foods and equipment must now fit within the strict limitations of space determined by that container, or by how many "units" or containers you are capable and willing to transport or carry. Descriptive—yet essential—terms must be small, compact, and lightweight. The containers should be lightweight and compact, yet have enough room in them for the items you need. They should be sturdy enough to withstand rough handling and adverse conditions. They should have sturdy handles. If possible, they should be waterproof. However, don't wait to start assembling your kits until you have perfect containers. Start now with whatever you have: polyethylene buckets with tight-fitting lids, suitcases, or even cardboard boxes. Even though it might not meet the ideal criteria, in this instance, something is much better than nothing. You can always improve and upgrade your kit containers later.

No single type of container meets all the needs of everyone. Try to use containers that are best suited to each individual's capabilities or limitations. Take into account each person's particular needs, such as age, size, health, and strength. Consider carefully how much each kit will weigh and whether or not the person will be able to carry it without too much trouble. Most likely your completed kit will consist of two "units": one for foods, supplies, and equipment; the second for water. You never know how far or how long a kit might have to be carried. For example, a backpack on a frame might suit a strong teenage boy, while a sturdy suitcase with a secure handle and wheels would be a more practical solution for a grandmother in her sixties.

Don't try to cram supplies for your entire family into one large container. If you do, you may not be able to move it when a critical situation arises. The contents of a 72-hour kit should be limited to suit the requirements for just one person.

Just Begin, Then Upgrade

MY FIRST EMERGENCY KIT

I started my first emergency kit in a large wooden footlocker, complete with heavy rope handles and a metal hasp. I regularly accumulated supplies in this box, and from time to time, I would lift the lid and gaze at the contents, enjoying the feeling of security it gave me. Then one day we decided to have an evacuation drill. When it came time to move the footlocker, I couldn't even budge it. In fact, it was so heavy that I probably couldn't have moved it even if it had been on wheels. We quickly learned that we needed to have a smaller, separate container for each member of our family.

When choosing a container for your kits, don't worry that you find the perfect one the first time you look. It doesn't have to be perfect. You can always change your mind or find a better one. I have upgraded and changed our containers several times. I'm always looking for new ideas that improve on what I have. Your evacuation kits are not created to store and forget. You'll need to update and replenish all perishable items regularly. Most likely, the clothing will need to be upgraded and changed to fit. (That's a polite way of saying it probably doesn't fit anymore. It's much better to replace it than have to do without.) Upgrade and replenish time is the time to get a better container.

Container Options

The following are options that could be used for your emergency kits. I have graded them according to how practically suited they are for the purpose of a 72-hour evacuation kit.

Recommended—Very well suited for the purpose.

Good—This will function acceptably.

Okay—You can make-do with this, but another container would probably be better. Plan to upgrade as soon as you can.

Not recommended—This does not suit the purpose.

Polyethylene Buckets: **Recommended**

Polyethylene buckets, in my opinion, are one of the best choices for a 72-hour kit. Six-gallon buckets with sturdy handles and snug-fitting lids are almost perfect. They are large enough to contain all the essential items for one adult, stack well, and are usually are reasonably priced. They are waterproof and versatile enough, once at a shelter, to carry water, or to be used as a seat, wash basin, or even a toilet if needed. I strongly recommend that each family have at least one bucket, even if a variety of other containers are used for your main kits.

Most hardware stores or emergency-preparedness outlets that stock these buckets carry a resin-type wrench, which quickly and efficiently opens the lids. It can easily be securely lashed to the handle of one of your buckets or duct-taped to the outside. (Don't pack the wrench inside with the rest of your supplies; that would pretty much defeat the purpose of having it.)

Many bakeries, doughnut shops, and supermarket bakeries have used buckets available. Originally they contained baking mixes and frosting. Many outlets will save them for you if you ask. Some are free; some are minimally priced. Be sure to get ones with lids that fit. You may need to wash the buckets. Try to get buckets that contained only frosting or cookie dough or other good-smelling foods, rather than pickle relish or hot peppers.

Some residual odors cannot be washed out of plastic. I suppose socks that smell like pickle relish would still work—maybe.

Plastic Storage Tubs: **Recommended**

The 10/20-gallon rectangular storage tubs with carrying handles are excellent container choices. They are available in the housewares or closet organizer section of most hardware and discount department stores. Select the kind that have snug-fitting, snap-lock lids that tend to make them water resistant. They stack well and could be used to carry water (though it probably would be more difficult than in a bucket; put the lid on to avoid splashing water). Avoid the brittle, see-through plastic containers with slip-on lids that resemble shoeboxes. Don't use tubs much larger than 18–20 gallons because when full they would be too heavy to carry.

Backpacks: **Recommended to Good**

Backpacks can be excellent containers for an emergency kit. Camping and backpacking packs that are sturdily made and have been created to withstand the rigors of bad weather and rough handling are recommended to use for a 72-hour kit. Most are easy to carry and are water repellent. Note that this is not the same as being waterproof. If a backpack with a backpacking frame is used, you could expand your kit capacity by including a sleeping bag or bedroll, along with additional equipment, such as backpacking tents, stoves, lanterns, and so on. Fully loaded, a frame-type backpack can weigh 60–80 pounds. Keep it lightweight. Backpacks with frames are not suitable for small children or the elderly.

School-type backpacks are one of the most popular containers used for evacuation kits and may or may not be recommended, depending on the design. The features that would deny them a high recommendation are their smaller size, zippers that open too widely, and poor-quality construction. Some backpacks just don't have the capacity to hold all the supplies a good evacuation kit will require. On the other hand, I've seen some that will hold forty pounds of textbooks, a jacket, sack lunch, school supplies, and still have room for art projects and show-and-tell items. These kinds may be plenty large enough, especially when you consider all the pockets on every surface. Some even have wheels and handles. To get all those books in and out, manufacturers often put zippers that stretch from one bottom corner up and around and down to the opposite bottom corner. This is good for books, but it's not so good for evacuation kits because all your supplies will fall out anytime you open it up. To get around this problem, you can fasten big, sturdy safety pins over the zipper teeth near the top of the backpack as zipper stops. Make sure a school-type backpack is well built, made of quality materials with sewn—not glued—seams, and that it can be securely closed. If it meets these conditions, then I can recommend it. If not, use it to get started and upgrade later.

Pack size and style should be adapted for the individual. Small children usually can manage backpacks more readily than most other container choices. If applicable, review the following family options segment before making your final decision on which option to pursue.

Backpacks and backpack units hang more easily than they stack. For example, sturdy hooks in a mudroom or garage are useful for keeping them accessible, yet out of the way. Waterproofing is an issue to deal with if backpacks are the kit container you choose.

Duffel Bags: Good

Heavy-duty, shoulder-strap-style duffel bags or gym bags make fairly good emergency kit containers. Some are water-repellent, and they usually are quite sturdy. Many have wheels and a handle, as well as quality zippers and multiple compartments. I can give these a "recommended" grade. I don't recommend the drawstring bags like those used for laundry, since they can be cumbersome and difficult to carry.

Luggage: Good to Recommended

Soft-sided luggage would be the type least recommended.

Check out the luggage section in a good discount department store. You'll find suitcases and baggage in all sorts of sizes and for all sorts of purposes, most of which adapt very well for use as an evacuation kit. Keep in mind, though, that if you fill a giant suitcase to the brim, it will be too heavy for most people to carry. Just because you *can* choose the largest suitcase known to man, and just because you *can* stuff it to near-exploding with supplies, does not mean you *should*. Remember, lightweight and portable are the keys. Wheels are very helpful. On any suitcase, make sure that the handles are secure. If the strength of the locking mechanism is questionable, strapping or tying the suitcase closed increases the stability. On the other hand, it also makes it more difficult to update each year. Most suitcases are not water-repellent or waterproof. Use heavy untreated trash bags inside the suitcase to keep the items protected from water.

PERSONAL EXPERIENCE WITH LUGGAGE

We are a senior couple. Both of us have back problems. We resolved our 72-hour kit dilemma with suitcases that have expanding handles and extra sturdy wheels. The key stays on our key ring.

—M. J., Sandy, Utah

Wheeled carry-on cases with retractable handles are generally a really good size for a 72-hour kit. Sometimes these are called Travelers. They're usually big enough (when fully expanded) to carry all your supplies, yet not so heavy that you can't lift them. I recommend them.

Tote Bags: Okay

Tote bags can be used for emergency kits if they can be closed securely, although they are usually not very sturdy. Most tote bags would usually be considered too small for a kit container. If you use a tote bag, make sure that the handles are securely fastened to the bag. A tote bag might be used for a child's kit. They are definitely not waterproof.

Produce Boxes: Okay

A sturdy, waxed produce box with handle holes can be used as a makeshift kit container. It's adequate to start with, but you should replace it with a better choice as soon as possible. Boxes are on the list only because they are a great choice if you want to start your evacuation kit right this minute. Boxes are affordable, and boxes are available. Other than that, they're not so great. Cardboard boxes are not waterproof at all. If one gets wet, it will fall apart. It will help provide some protection against water if you place the contents of your kit in a heavy-duty, plastic trash bag inside the box and then put the whole box into another trash bag. Strapping or tying would increase the stability of the box, and the tape or rope could function as a handle if you fasten it that way.

Trunks, Footlockers, and Ammunition Boxes: Not recommended

I do not recommend using these for emergency kits. They are much too heavy and unmanageable for one person to move. Also, their lids usually do not fit securely.

Garbage Cans: Not recommended.

Metal, plastic, or rubber garbage cans don't make good emergency kit containers. They become much too heavy and unwieldy, even if they have wheels. Many people have recommended using them, but a 30-gallon can full of supplies can weigh up to two hundred pounds and requires a hand truck and a moving crew to move it. They would be almost impossible to get into a car. Another problem with using a garbage can as a kit container is getting to the supplies at the bottom of the can once you're in a shelter. Also, they are not waterproof. In the confusion of trying to transport or use them in an evacuation area, the lids could be easily knocked off.

PERSONAL EXPERIENCE
WITH GARBAGE CANS

During a mock disaster and evacuation drill in the summer of 1985, the following "garbage-can incident" was reported by a Red Cross director in Provo, Utah. The mock "evacuation center" was established. As the drill progressed, it was brought to the attention of the authorities that an elderly, disabled lady, who lived across the street from the command center, required help to evacuate. Three male volunteers were sent to "rescue" her. It took several more volunteers to bring out her evacuation kit. Their response was, "It weighed a ton!" "It" was a thirty-gallon garbage can, filled to the brim!

A combination of units may work better for a family than individual kits.

Family Options

When planning kits for a family or a multimember household, a combination of units may better suit your needs than individual kits. (Read the sections on foods, water, and equipment before making final decisions.) Make individual kits for each individual family member, including only personal clothing items and minimal supplies such as a blanket, flashlight and batteries, morale boosters, trial-sized personal hygiene supplies, and so on.

Then create food kits for the whole family in one or two buckets, including whatever fuel options and utensils will be required for those food choices. This provides a greater quantity of food. In a parent's kit or additional container, include other essentials such as the battery-powered radio, spare batteries, first-aid supplies, and the other essential miscellaneous items. Adapt and adjust your kits as the family grows and changes.

Beware of Rumors

Emergency preparations can easily be driven by rumor, fads, or panic. Before you let yourself get all stirred up, use your head and think! I heard one the other day: "Never use a bucket as a kit if you have small children because you can't carry a bucket and carry your child—you'll have to leave one or the other behind." Talk about absurd!

First, if your kits are ready and waiting to be grabbed in an emergency, you'll have plenty of time to put both your kit and your kid in the car, or in the stroller, or the wagon, or on whatever mode of transportation *you've already decided on.* Second, it should be obvious from my recommendations above that buckets make much better containers than many other options. In personal preparedness, the operative word is *personal* (unless of course you're making a different point, and then the operative word is *preparedness.*) You choose which container—of all the good choices—will best fit your needs, and you find the ways to make it work. Before you jump on any

STORE KITS FOR EASY RETRIEVAL

On a wet, blustery winter night in 1984, some friends of ours heard sirens. Suddenly a policeman pounded on their door. "You have just five minutes to get out," he said. "There's a fire in the chemical plant just west of here. Grab your family and leave." Acrid smoke was already beginning to fill the air. They wanted to take their emergency kits, which were stored under the stairs in the basement. Unfortunately, they quickly discovered other objects had gotten piled on top of and in front of the kits. They couldn't take the time required to dig the kits out. Ultimately, they picked up their children, wrapped them in quilts, jumped in the car, and drove off.

faddish bandwagon, think it through first, and then sensibly make up your own mind.

Keep Your Kits Accessible

A kit is rendered useless unless you can get to it! Keep your kits where you can grab them at a moment's notice. Find an unobtrusive yet safe and convenient spot. Assess your home or apartment from a structural standpoint. The storage area should be as sturdy as possible. For example, a closet is a good selection in an earthquake prone area because of the support of the wall studs. Our family's kits in buckets are stacked in a closet near our front door. One family I know has their kits in backpacks, which hang on hooks near their back door. A widowed senior citizen keeps her suitcase kit in a small space at the end of a kitchen cupboard. Still another family adjusted the rod and shelf in a family room closet. All of their kits fit in one end of that closet.

Another alternative might be to find a location to keep your kits outside of your living quarters, such as in the garage, stacked neatly and unencumbered by a door. Not by the car entrance door, however. It could prove to be too difficult to get open in some circumstances. Or perhaps a weatherproof, aluminum utility shed on your property, away from the main house, would work.

Label Your Kits

Be sure to label your kits with your name and phone number. (Or use your first initial and last name. Don't use your address, for security purposes.) Use indelible marking pens, and make the writing as bright, permanent, and easily identifiable as possible. This will help you to keep track of your kits in an evacuation center, where many people could have kits similar to yours. In all the chaos and confusion, one kit can easily look like another. You might even decorate your kits for easy identification. This could also help brighten a dreary evacuation center. You may wish to use a slogan, such as "This too shall pass." Don't underestimate the positive psychological influence this can have on you and others. It would probably be wise to label the items in your kit as well. In the long run, it could prevent confusion and loss of property in a crowded shelter.

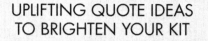

UPLIFTING QUOTE IDEAS TO BRIGHTEN YOUR KIT

- This too shall pass.
- My other evacuation kit is a Winnebago.
- No one ever said it was going to be easy, but this is ridiculous!
- Have bucket, will travel.
- I'm just here for the food.
- You know, Toto, I don't think we're in Kansas anymore.
- The sun will come out tomorrow.

What if Someone Is Away from Home?

There's always the chance that one or two persons may be the only ones at home when a crisis occurs. They will have to get the kits out and to the evacuation center (or to a predetermined family meeting place). A wagon or other conveyance in good repair may be a necessity to transport a number of kits, particularly if the owner of the kit is not there to carry it. If others are away from home when you are evacuated, take their kits with you. As soon as humanly possible, separated family members will be reunited, with the help of the authorities, friends, and neighbors. At that point, the missing family members will need their kits for the rest of their stay in the shelter. (See "What if You Have to Walk Out?" in chapter 11.) In a situation with latchkey children it is critical to work this problem through with your Care-in-a-Crisis group members. (See chapter 9.)

The "Don't Forget" List

> *A "Don't Forget" list should be a permanent part of the kit.*

On the list, include items you must remember to take with you but are using each day so that they can't be put into your kit now, such as eyeglasses, prescription medicines, shoes, or special needs. Solidly tape the list to the container with duct tape, strapping tape, or some other tape that does not readily peel off or lose its adhesiveness with time or humidity. In extreme trauma, you can even forget your own name. Things such as keys and wallets may seem extreme now, but should the occasion arise, such a list could prove to be a lifesaver. Write down the location of the items as well so that you will be able to find them immediately, or so that if someone outside your family is helping you evacuate, they will be able to quickly find them. If your kit is assembled, you will usually have time to quickly gather these few critical items.

Create a Car Kit

In today's commuting lifestyle, many of you spend a great deal of time in automobiles or at work away from home. The reason to have a kit in the car is that should you be stranded for any reason you would not be helpless. It does not even have to be a major disaster. In a land laced by freeways and belt routes and plagued with traffic congestion, it can be a commonplace occurrence to be caught in the gridlock, sometimes for hours at a time. Anyone traveling any distance, especially with children, should always place a top priority on a car kit. The probability of facing an evacuation while at your workplace is real. Should the crisis be of major proportions, you may be required to walk out.

This type of kit is in *addition* to any emergency tool or equipment kit you choose to keep in the trunk.

I recommend that the kit container for your car be a backpack, so that regardless of the circumstances, you are able to care for yourself and walk, with supplies that will sustain you. The scope of a car kit is smaller than a 72-hour evacuation kit. The weather and seasonal changes in your area will affect the kinds of foods as well as emergency clothing that you include. For example, in areas with extremely cold winters where you might actually be trapped in your car, consider including a heat source such as chemical hand or foot warmers, canned fuel, and a small portable stove, along with envelopes of instant soup or hot cocoa. (Not for use inside the car, of course. Place it on the ground outside or on the hood of the car.) In hot climates, you'll need to include more water. The fluctuating temperatures in a car's trunk will cause faster deterioration than in a kit kept in a home. Foods containing chocolate or other ingredients that melt easily are not good choices.

Determine how many people are in the car most of the time. This will help you determine the contents and amount of supplies in your car kit. If the car is used by an individual commuting, assess the commute with the same care as the neighborhood evaluation. If the travelers are mostly a mother and children, adapt the kits, contents, and amounts accordingly. A few items to consider are:

- Bottled water
- Sturdy walking shoes and socks
- Poncho
- Small first-aid kit
- Flashlight, spare batteries
- Moist towelettes
- Charger for cell phone
- Energy foods/bars
- Trail mix

- Ready-to-eat, pop-top canned foods
- Small battery-powered radio, extra batteries
- Space blanket/fleece throw
- Small bottle of aspirin or pain reliever
- Small pad of paper and pencil—to be able to leave a note on the car saying where you have gone and the date and time.
- Small folding umbrella

Mini-Desk Pack

The chances of being forced to evacuate from your workplace are as great as at home. Think about your work situation, especially if you rely on public transportation to get to and from work. You might have to walk out. Do you have a locker or a desk drawer where it would be permissible to maintain a small emergency kit? This could prove to be critical if you are diabetic or hyperglycemic. Many companies are now encouraging and assisting employees to have a plan in place at the workplace in case of an emergency. Do not use this kit as a replacement on the days you forget your lunch! A school-type backpack or small duffel bag is a good work-kit option. One point, especially for women who usually wear high heels to work, so make sure heavy socks and walking shoes (that are already broken in) are part of your kit. It will certainly make it easier if you have to walk any distance. The list of suggested items for a car kit is also a good list to consider for an at-work kit.

At School

Contact other parents and get involved with the PTA to insure as much security as possible for the children while they are at school. Many parent groups are compiling simple lists of suggested items to be included in a mini-pack for each child, per classroom. This list, which includes suggestions for just a few practical foods such as granola bars or energy bars and a space blanket, is one of the first things sent home at the beginning of each year. In one school district in San Jose, California, these mini-packs are collected at the beginning of the year, put into a garbage can that is then duct-taped closed, and tucked in a corner of the room. Each class has a flashlight that hangs on a hook and a backpack full of first-aid supplies so the teacher can grab them in a rush if needed. The faculty is assigned different responsibilities. And they have drills. Another school reported that parents also included in the child's mini-pack a picture of the parents and/or family and a short, encouraging letter. These were returned sealed, with the mini-pack to be opened only if needed. The packs are sent home with the child at the end of the school year. One word of caution: make sure parents understand the foods are to be non-perishable. One school reported a "strong aroma" that caused a small crisis in one classroom until the source could be tracked down. It turned out to be some very perishable food in one of the children's kits.

For older children in junior high and high school where the students are more independent, a small kit in an unobtrusive container could remain undetected even when a locker door was open. No-snitch rules must apply to the food in the kit, but that's no guarantee that snitching won't happen. You may have to send replacements several times a year for your peace of mind.

Many schools and school districts have very detailed plans for dealing with emergencies of all sorts, including how to get children home, or what to do with them if going home isn't an option. Call your local principal or district office to see what plans they have in place. It will either relieve your mind to know their plans or galvanize you to action if your school has not taken any steps for preparedness.

Do You Have Pets?

If you have pets, take as many precautions as possible to insure their survival. As part of your planning sessions, write a list of pet "to-do's" and "must-haves." As a general rule, pets are not allowed inside shelters (excluding service animals) due to health regulations. If you plan on taking your pet with you and keeping it outside the shelter, you will need to have a 72-hour pet kit, consisting of food, water, leashes, kennel or cage, and some plans as to how to take care of droppings. Consider taking a tent along to the shelter. If necessary, you could stay in it outside the shelter with your animals. Don't simply turn your animals loose, thinking they can fend for themselves. In cases of disasters such as earthquakes or hurricanes, roving animals may be destroyed in order to prevent more problems and the spread of disease.

> *Pet owners will need to have*
> *a 72-hour pet kit.*

CHAPTER THREE

MEALS FROM A KIT

During a crisis or evacuation period, the right types of foods are critical. A stress situation demands more energy than normal, which is why in many instances foods high in calories, even empty calories, are recommended for survival. Practical advance preparation can insure a relatively good balance of nutrition along with the necessary high calories.

People can live for several days without food if they have water to drink. However, most of us are accustomed to regular meals and plenty of food. The emergency itself will be enough to deal with. There is no need to compound the difficulty with headaches, irritability, and discomfort that lack of food will create. In fact, failure to provide proper nourishment for yourself could increase someone else's burden.

Besides providing nourishment, the eating of "meals" during an emergency has a positive psychological effect. It brings some order to an otherwise chaotic time, and it helps people feel that they do have some control over a difficult situation.

> *The eating of "meals" during an emergency has a positive psychological effect.*

Consider the Pros, Cons, and Problems

Of course, eventually food may be provided in an evacuation center during an emergency. However, keep in mind the ever-present problem of lag time during a crisis. Days may pass before the courtesy kitchen can be brought in, be set up, and begin to function. During lag time, *without proper provisions,* chaos that normally could be coped with could turn into an absolute nightmare for anyone, particularly those with special dietary needs. Also, food in an evacuation center is usually donated by individuals, restaurants, and canneries. Even if foods were immediately supplied, this presents a problem for diabetics, hypoglycemics, and others with dietary restrictions. There are usually no options for eliminating sugar, salt, or other additives from your diet. Those with severe food allergies cannot take the chance of eating totally from a public food line. For example, I am severely allergic to nuts. If someone even cut a bologna sandwich in half with a knife or on the cutting board that had previously been used to make a peanut butter sandwich, it could be deadly for me. I have to provide more food for myself in my emergency kit than most people because it may prove to be too risky to eat food that I cannot be sure is safe for me.

Give special attention to food problems that may arise. *Beforehand,* assess and find solutions to the dietary needs of babies, toddlers, invalids, the elderly, diabetics, hypoglycemics, those people with severe allergies, and those on no/low-sodium diets. If someone in your family has a critical dietary need, prepare now, and prepare for a longer span of time than you might otherwise need to.

Plan Now—the Right Way

Planning *now* assures existing as close to normalcy as possible. Because foods will comprise the bulk of your kit, be extremely careful in planning which foods to take and how much. Balanced meals are not the main concern in this instance. High calories along with good nutrition are what to look for. Foods that are *lightweight, compact,* and that *require no refrigeration, preparation, or cooking* are best suited for an evacuation kit. Concentrated foods such as high-energy trail bars are good choices. Many of the nutritious staple items you already have in your home such as flour, grains, beans, and pasta, absolutely *will not* function in an emergency kit. They are bulky and require too much preparation.

The type, style, and food packaging that you choose to go in your kit will determine the kind of utensils and equipment required. For example, compare the differences between regular cans of pork and beans and granola bars. With the pork and beans, you must also pack a can opener and a spoon, and ideally, a bowl to eat from and a pan to heat them in. This is not necessarily bad. Just remember, a little weight can add up quickly. This one point alone will determine a major portion of the bulk and weight of your kit. Keep in mind that the circumstances of the evacuation as well as the space in your container are extremely limiting factors.

Food for a Baby or Toddler

Infants and small children may not be able to eat unfamiliar food in a shelter situation. I have discussed these situations with several Red Cross directors, and each has emphasized that one of the greatest problems, in a major crisis involving several days and many people is trying to feed babies and small children. Unfamiliar food is very difficult on their tiny systems. If you have a baby or toddler, you will need to provide for their special needs. If your baby is eating solid food, but not all the regular foods an adult eats, you will need to include some kind of baby food. The drawbacks to baby food in jars are the weight and the glass. You can deal with the glass by making sure the jars are padded and protected from breakage, or choose the kind in the plastic containers. Instant dry foods such as cereal, fruits, and vegetables are all available without the disadvantages of glass jars. These must be reconstituted with water, but even cold water would do in a pinch. Whatever you use, be sure that they are foods your child has eaten before and likes. You could also include bottled juices and aseptic milk if your child is used to having a bottle throughout the day.

Nursing mothers should consider the possibility that because of the stress brought on by the emergency, they might not be able to produce enough milk for their babies. If you are a nursing mother (or soon-to-be-nursing mother), you should include some liquid formula in your kit in case you are unable to nurse. Even though powdered formula weighs less, you may not be able to use it if water is not available. Think about including both liquid and powdered formula in your kit. Don't forget baby bottles and nipples.

Foods Suitable for Evacuation Kits

You will be surprised at the wide variety of foods that are suitable for emergency kits. The majority of them are available at your local supermarkets. Others may be available at sporting goods outlets or health food stores. Remember, though, an evacuation shelter is not a good place to try new, unusual foods. When possible, stick to simple foods and tastes that you are accustomed to.

Consider a combination of the following suggested foods to meet your needs:

Stress Foods: Such foods as hard candy, chocolate, energy bars, and sugared dry cereal are known as stress foods. These are a necessity in a 72-hour kit. In stressful situations, people require an increased caloric intake to meet the extraordinary demands for energy. Stress foods meet the requirements for survival, not for a balanced diet. They are small and compact and should be liberally tucked into tiny places throughout your evacuation kit. They also help boost morale. If you can't eat sugar because of dietary restrictions, try the diabetic candies made with artificial sweeteners.

Compressed Food Bars: Compressed food bars, such as granola bars and trail bars, are excellent for use in emergency kits. They are small, store well, are lightweight, taste good, and are fairly nutritious and high in calories.

Survival Drink Mixes: These drink mixes are a blend of proteins, vitamins, and minerals which can be mixed with liquid. Available at emergency preparedness outlets, this type of mix could be used as *part* of your food. Add a variety and volume of solid foods for more normalcy later as you upgrade your kits. You will need water to mix it with.

Trail Mixes: Trail mixes are mixtures of such ingredients as granola, nuts, seeds, and dried fruits. They taste good, and they are high in calories and nutrition. Trail mixes can become rancid after a few months, especially if kept in a hot location. Replace them several times a year.

Dried Foods: Dried foods, especially meat and fruit, are fine for 72-hour kits. They taste good, are nutritious, and are satisfying. One problem with jerky is that it may make you thirsty. Dried fruit is not the same as dehydrated fruit, which is not recommended.

Freeze-Dried Foods: Freeze-dried foods are excellent additions to evacuation kits. You may be familiar with these as backpacking foods found in sporting goods stores. Many are available in supermarkets, as well. They are lightweight and tasty, but water is needed for their reconstitution. If necessary, they can be reconstituted with cold water. Some freeze-dried foods come in larger #2 cans. If those cans are too large and bulky for your particular kit, think about repackaging the food into something smaller, such as Ziploc bags or small plastic food containers.

Instant Soups: Envelopes of instant soups are compact and excellent for 72-hour kits. They provide nourishment and if necessary could be fixed in a cup of cold water.

Instant Meals: You might include such "instant" meals as cups of noodles, cups of casseroles, and so on. These "meals" are usually freeze-dried and will reconstitute immediately with hot water. In dire straits, cold water will work. They are an excellent consideration for 72-hour kits.

Shelf-Stable Foods: "Shelf stable" refers to retort processing, which stabilizes the foods so that they require no refrigeration. They are usually packaged in plastic pouches. Many of them are marketed as microwave meals, similar to frozen TV dinners; however, these are found on the shelf in the supermarket instead of the freezer case. You can find shelf-stable lunch meals like tuna, ham, and chicken salad also. These kinds of meals make it easy to have high-quality protein in your 72-hour kit meals.

For better space efficiency in your kit, consider discarding the outer cardboard packaging. A goal for a 72-hour kit would be to provide a variety of tasty and nutritious foods, without the bulk or weight of canned foods. They could be heated quickly or eaten cold if necessary.

Meals Ready to Eat: The current version of C rations, MREs, are the shelf-stable foods designed for the armed services. Most come as single servings, in a multilayered foil or plastic pouch. However, if you consider using MREs try several first, particularly if they are the armed services variety. Some are good; some are not so good. Many times it is necessary to buy a case or half case. Be cautious: if a sales price sounds too good to be true, you may end up with seventy-two of the same variety. MREs usually are available at emergency preparedness outlets, sporting good stores, and surplus outlets.

MRE heater bags are also available. They somewhat resemble a plastic mailing envelope. A cardboard heater in the bottom is chemically activated when water is added; therefore you need to have additional water with your kits to make them work. Space may be an issue, since each heater can only be used once. They become very hot, so children should not be allowed to use them without supervision.

Instant Cereals/Instant Breakfasts: The variety of instant cereal packets and instant breakfasts available are a boon to evacuation kits. They provide relatively good food value, and could be eaten cold if necessary.

Instant Milk: Consider including small packets of instant milk. It could be used to fortify other foods for added nutrition, or it could be used alone. The key is instant, not regular non-fat dry milk. Put serving-size portions in resealable zipper bags. Just add water to the zipper bag, seal it, and shake to reconstitute the milk.

Snack-Sized or Single-Serving Canned Goods: Pull-top snack-sized canned goods are small and make good additions to evacuation kits. Such items as gelatins, fruit cups, puddings, and tapioca could provide food value, familiar taste, and bulk to the diet. The smallest sized cans of such items as corned beef, deviled ham, Vienna sausages, and luncheon meat fit the parameters for a kit. Soups, pork and beans, vegetables, and fruits are available in single-serving size with pull-tops. One advantage of these foods is they are already processed and could be eaten cold. The "flat size" (approximately 6 ounces) of foods such as chicken, tuna, or pineapple works well. A can opener may be required if the cans don't have pop-tops. Weight and lack of space will be the problems of canned foods. Consider using a few canned items in a smaller ratio to other lighter types of foods in your kit.

Dietary Supplements: Liquid dietary supplements such as *Ensure* and similar single-serving supplements, recommended by many doctors for older patients, are a source of nutrition in a can. They could be considered as a good option for an evacuation kit. Weight might be a problem, but a few might work well, and not just for seniors. They feature a pull-top opening. You'll still want some solid food in your kit.

Snack Foods: Small, packaged snack foods work well in evacuation kits. Snack-pack cheese and crackers, snack-pack peanut butter and crackers, roasted nuts (in cellophane or foil packages), or small variety-pack dry or sugared cereals are a few examples. Be aware of their flimsy packaging and be careful how you stuff them in your kits or you'll have crumbs everywhere. Some snack items such as nuts will have a short shelf life. Replace them regularly every four to six months, more frequently in humid climates.

Drink Mixes: Drink mixes add variety to a 72-hour kit. Try such items as hot chocolate mix or presweetened powdered fruit drinks. These usually come in small envelopes, so they fit easily in the kit. You'll need water to mix them with.

Liquid Beverages: Juices and milk are available in aseptic packaging. Often referred to as "soft cans," they come with a straw and require no refrigeration. These are perfect for use in emergency kits. Pouches may be easier to fit into kits, if you have a choice. You might also consider using small cans of juice that open with a pull-tab.

A 72-Hour Menu

Following are sample menus that could get one person through a 72-hour emergency. Although lacking the bulk of usual meals, they contain a good variety of food with sufficient calories and are fairly inexpensive. Note that although liquid is not shown in this menu, you must keep it in mind as you plan! You also must have it in addition to your food. Also note the difference in weight between the two sample menus.

Suggested 72-Hour Supermarket Food Menus

Sample #1

Item	Weight	Extra Water Required?	Calories per day	Amount for 72 hours	Cost for 72 hours ($)*
Pop Tarts	11 oz.	NO	420	6	1.79
Granola Bars	3 oz.	NO	120	3	0.78†
Cereal Bars	3.75 oz.	NO	180	3	1.41†
Cup O' Noodles	6.75 oz.	YES	290	3	1.77
Banana Chips	5 oz.	NO	750	3	4.47
Pork and Beans	8 oz.	NO	240	3	2.37
Sunflower Seeds	3.25 oz.	NO	170	3	1.47
Cracker Jacks	3.75 oz.	NO	120	3	1.19
TOTAL	44.5 oz. (2¾ lbs.)		2290		15.15

*Prices were accurate at the time of the survey in 2004
and are listed as examples only.

† Full box not required, price prorated.

Sample #2

Item	Weight	Extra Water Required?	Calories per day	Amount for 72 hours	Cost for 72 hours ($)*
Instant Oatmeal	4.5 oz.	YES	150	3	0.87†
Milk, aseptic	24 oz.	NO	120	3	1.09
Fruit Cup	13.5 oz.	NO	60	3	1.50†
Peanuts	9 oz.	NO	585	9 oz.	1.12
Ramen Noodles	9 oz.	YES	400	3	.75
Pudding	12 oz.	NO	160	3	1.10†
Lasagna MRE	30 oz.	NO	350	3	5.96
Fruit Roll-Up	1.5 oz.	NO	50	3	.84†
Cereal Bar	3.75 oz.	NO	180	3	1.42†
TOTAL	107.5 oz. (6¾ lbs.)		2055		14.65

*Prices were accurate at the time of the survey in 2004
and are listed as examples only.

† Full box not required, price pro-rated.

Supermarket Success with 72-Hour Foods

The following foods are listed to give you an immediate overview of some of the items that are readily available on supermarket shelves, their weight, calories, and approximate cost.

Canned Foods			
Item	Weight (oz.)	Calories	Cost ($)
Tuna	6.25	195	0.79
Corned Beef *Hormel*	12	720	2.09
Deviled Ham	2.5	—	0.98
Vienna Sausages *Libby*	5	180	0.59
Spam	7	1020	1.39
Pork and Beans *Van de Camp*	8	60 per 2 oz.	0.79
Spaghettios	15	160 per 7.5 oz.	0.59
Chili con Carne w/ Beans	15	240 per 7.5 oz.	0.99
Pudding *Snack Pak*	16 per 4	160	1.49
Peaches *Del Monte*	8.5	100 per 4.25 oz.	0.75
Jell-O Cups	14 per 4	100	1.19
Applesauce *Musselman's*	24 per 6	80	1.88
Soup *Hormel*	7.5	110	0.98
Lasagna *Top Shelf*	10	350	1.98
Beef Stew *Nalley*	7.5	—	1.09

CEREALS			
Item	Weight (oz.)	Calories	Cost ($)
Granola Bars *Quaker Chewy*	10 per 10	120 per 1	2.59
Granola Bars *Nature Valley*	10 per 12	120 per 1	2.39
Cereal Bars *NutriGrain*	10.4 per 8	140 per 1	2.85
Cereal Bars *Kudos*	7.5 per 6	180 per 1	2.85
Box Cereals *Snack Size*	10 boxes	100-210	3.29
Instant Oatmeal *Quake*r	15 per 10	150 per 1	2.89
Cream of Wheat, instant	12.5 per 10	130 per 1	2.89
Baby Cereal *Gerber*, trial	6 per 6	50 per .5 oz.	1.45
Granola *American Mills*	64	100 per .33 cup	5.98
Trail Mix	bulk	150 per oz.	2.99 per lb.
Cracker Jacks	3.75 per 3	120 per oz.	1.19
Pop Tarts	11 per 6	210 per 1	1.79
Peanuts, salted	bulk	585 per 3 oz.	1.98 per lb.
Peanuts, pull-top can, *Planters*	6.5	170 per oz.	1.59
Sunflower seeds shelled, Fisher's	3.25	170 per oz.	0.49

INSTANT MEALS			
Item	Weight (oz.)	Calories	Cost ($)
Cup O' Noodles *Nissin*	2.25	290	0.59
Top Ramen Noodles	3	200 per 1.5 oz.	0.25
Cup O' Soup *Lipton*	2.1 per 4	50 per 1	1.17
Noodle Soup *Campbell's*	1.33	140	0.69

DRIED, NOT DEHYDRATED			
Item	Weight (oz.)	Calories	Cost ($)
Banana Chips *Mariani*	5	150 per oz.	1.49
Pears *Mariani*	8	150 per 2 oz.	2.98
Apple Rings	6	150 per .25 cup	2.49
Raisins, canned *Sunmaid*	24	250 per .5 oz.	2.49
Beef Jerky *Smoky Mountain*	1	80	1.69

STRESS FOODS			
Item	Weight (oz.)	Calories	Cost ($)
Peppermint Candy *Brach's*	bulk	—	1.49 per lb.
Chocolate-covered Peanuts	bulk	—	2.99 per lb.

LIQUIDS			
Item	Weight (oz.)	Calories	Cost ($)
Capri Sun Juice, foil packets	67 per 10	—	2.79
Juice *Squeeze-It*	40 per 6	110 per 1	2.79
Pineapple *Dole*	36 per 6	100 per 1	1.99
Juicy Juice *Libby*	25 per 3	130 per 1	1.29
Milk, aseptic boxes	24 per 3	120 per 1	1.09
Instant Breakfast *Carnation*	10	220	1.09

MISCELLANEOUS			
Item	Weight (oz.)	Calories	Cost ($)
Peanut Butter *Skippy*	12	581 per 3 oz.	1.98
Apple Jelly	10	—	1.29
Cheese and Crackers *Handi-Snack*	1.1	—	0.39
Cheese and Pretzels *Handi-Snack*	1.02	—	0.39
Fruit Roll-Ups *Betty Crocker*	4 per 8	50 each	2.29
Instant Breakfast, add milk *Carnation*	12.6 per 10	130 without milk	3.79

Prices were accurate at the time of the survey in 2004
and are listed as examples only.

Foods Not Suitable for Evacuation Kits

Because 72-hour kits have such strict parameters for space and weight, there are many types of foods that are just not suitable at all for inclusion. The following kinds of food are *not* suitable for 72-hour kits:

Commercially Dehydrated Foods: Even though these are excellent products for "regular emergency preparedness," commercially dehydrated foods require a great deal of water for reconstitution, and they would be difficult to prepare properly in an evacuation situation. Labeled in many instances as "long-term storage items," these foods *cannot* be eaten as if they were dried foods. They must be reconstituted properly, which requires a great deal of hot water. They do not reconstitute very well without *hot* water, extensive soaking or cooking. They would be very difficult to use in an evacuation situation.

Bottled Foods: Bottled foods are too heavy and take up too much space to make them practical for emergency kits. Also, bottles break easily.

Commercially Canned Foods: Other than the small-sized canned goods previously discussed, commercially canned foods weigh too much and take up too much space. One government agency published a list of canned goods that they felt should be put in an evacuation kit. For two people, the weight of the cans of food alone was fifty-five pounds! This is just not practical. You might use canned goods to get started on your kits, but if you do, you should replace them with more compact foods as soon as possible. Don't forget to include a can opener.

Containers, Utensils, and Equipment

You will probably need to include some kind of utensils or other equipment in your kits, depending on the type of food you pack. Try to use as few as possible, as they add weight and take up space that could otherwise be used for food. The kinds of food you choose will directly affect the equipment or utensils you'll need. If something needs to be heated, you'll need a pan and spoon. Some food needs to be put in a bowl, or on a plate, or be eaten with a fork or spoon. Everyone should have a cup, at least. Review the food you are putting in your kit and determine what you'll need to fix or eat it. Heavyweight plasticware is lighter than metal forks and spoons but not as durable. The same is true for bowls, cups, and plates. The sturdy disposable plastic variety is lighter, but the regular items will last longer. You decide. I'm not recommending that you pack enough plastic ware to throw out your utensils after each meal; that would take much too much space. With care, one set of heavy-duty plastic ware could conceivably last 72 hours or longer. Possibly. Another less-breakable idea is to use camping nested utensils. A metal multiuse sierra cup could function as a cup, bowl, plate and even mini-saucepan, though not all at the same time. (Since they nest together, you could include several in a kit.) An aluminum pie pan would also serve as a plate or bowl.

Some of your food may need to be transferred from its original packaging into small containers more suited to your 72-hour kit. Small Rubbermaid- or Tupperware-type products with tight-fitting lids are ideal. You can also use small, plastic freezer containers. Heavy-gauge sandwich or freezer bags could work, though they're not the best, since mice, moths, and weevil can get into them, or the product in them could easily be smashed. Aluminum foil and paper bags are poor choices for holding kit foods because they are just too flimsy.

Stove Options

Some of the food you choose to put in your kit may require heating to make it edible or tolerable. Obviously you can't have hot chocolate without the hot. In that case, you have to provide a source to do that. It's important to note, though, that open flames of any size or configuration may not be allowed inside an evacuation shelter. Before you strike a single match, you'll want to check the regulations for the building. If you have the option, you could take a stove outside to heat your hot chocolate.

> *Many stove options fit the size and weight restrictions of emergency kits.*

That said, there are many stove options that fit the size and weight restrictions of emergency kits. The extremely small winged-tab or folding stoves that use heat tabs for fuel are well suited for this purpose. Two heat tabs on top of each other in a winged stove will heat a cup of water to boiling in a short amount of time: five or six minutes. Canned Heat and the accompanying folding Sterno stoves are good choices. Small backpacking stoves that use canisters of fuel also work, although they may weigh more and take up more space. (Not necessarily though; you can find some pretty small, lightweight stoves on the market. The weight is in the fuel canister more than in the stove.) If you don't have any food in your emergency kit that needs to be heated, you can dispense with a stove and fuel altogether. However, warm food can go a long way to calming down frightened, worried people. You may wish to include a small cooking source and the food supplies for warm drinks or soup just for the soothing influence they can have.

Equipment Suggestions

Here are some equipment and utensils to consider for your kit. You may not need all of these things, or you may need more than you see listed here. Use this list to jog your mind as to your needs.

- Small cooking pots
- Spoons, forks, and knives (some plastic, some metal)
- Nesting, camp-style knife, fork, and spoon sets
- Sierra cups (metal camping/backpacking cups that you can heat food in or drink from)
- Small, trial-sized bottle of dish soap
- Hot pad (a wash cloth can serve a dual purpose)

- Can opener (the small GI type works well)
- Matches in waterproof container
- Small backpacking stove with fuel canister
- Canned solid fuel (such as Sterno) and folding stove
- Heat tablets and winged-tab stove or folding stove

Practice Sessions

Before a critical situation forces you from home, it is important to practice preparing and eating meals from the kind of food you have included in your evacuation kits. A meal for one person might consist entirely of a granola bar, three graham crackers, half a cup of raisins, and a hot drink from a mix. You may want to find out what a normally hot food tastes like prepared with cold water. A practice session might seem more real if it is held outside your home. (No one should be able to go home and eat more after the practice session. That defeats the experiment.) As your family eats, you will learn what tastes good and what doesn't, and what works and what doesn't. This will help you make adjustments in what you include or delete from your kits.

If you are including a small folding stove in your kits, try cooking a meal on it. This will help you learn how to use the stove before you have to in an emergency. Every member of your family should be taught safety precautions in using the stove. For example, the instant a lit match touches a heat tab, the tab will ignite, although you may not be able to see it burning. A person not aware of this could easily be burned. Be sure to put the stove on a stable, level surface.

Holding practice sessions with household members is one of the most important parts of gaining realistic understanding and experience of what it means to prepare meals with food and equipment in your kit.

Another note from my experiences: for several weeks after the Loma Prieta earthquake, I was a guest on many radio talk shows. One of the questions I was asked, almost without fail, was, "Barbara, you supposedly were prepared; did you learn anything? Did your kits provide adequately for you?" Yes, I learned something. Even though we did not have to live out of our kits during the aftermath, I gave them a great deal of thought and deliberation, since at any minute during those first harrowing days, I may have needed to grab them and get out. After a few weeks passed and I got ready to put the kits away in the closet, I concluded that the meager quantities of food I had in our kits would be just survival amounts. What was needed was *more:* more food, more water, more bulk, more normalcy. Since there are only two members in my household now, I immediately began a third unit: a bucket that contains as much regular food as I could get into it and still carry it—items such as snack-pack fruits and puddings, cup-of-casseroles (freeze-dried meals), cup-of-soups, and so on. Still lightweight, still compact, but *more.*

A major problem, in my opinion, with most commercial kits is that the quality and quantity of the bulk in foods is lacking. Even though they provide sufficient calories, three survival bars as your "complete food supply for three days" does not qualify as adequate. If you have purchased your kit ready-made, it is critical that you realistically consider how "meals" are defined in your kit. Augment any insufficient food supplies with more, more, and more. You won't be sorry.

CHAPTER FOUR

WATER: A CRITICAL INGREDIENT

During an evacuation, water may or may not be available. The greater the severity of the crisis, the greater the probability that normal water supplies will be interrupted. Usually, water can be found at an evacuation shelter, but once again lag time can affect how soon and how much. Also, community water supplies may have become polluted; this is a common occurrence after a major earthquake or storm. If electrical power is out, the pumps that ordinarily bring water through the system may not be working. It may take time to bring in large water trucks. After Katrina devastated Louisiana in 2005, some areas were without water for over a week.

There are two areas of concern when dealing with water and being evacuated: (1) coping with lag time, and (2) having a suitable container in which to carry water at the evacuation shelter area.

Coping with Lag Time

The purpose for a *water unit* as part of but in addition to your 72-hour kit is to allow you to be able to cope without a normal water supply during lag time in an evacuation area. Once a water supply is established, the concern lessens somewhat. Until then you need to have a sufficient amount to last until an adequate water supply can be established.

The minimum requirement for *drinking* water is six quarts per person for 72 hours (three days). This much water weighs 12 pounds. Other needs, such as brushing teeth and preparing foods, usually require an additional two quarts per person per day. When planning for a family, you might think about including a 5-gallon water jug with a spigot. When full, it weighs forty pounds. This would not be difficult if you had a suitcase tote or something with wheels to move it about.

How Much Should You Carry?

When deciding how much water to take with you, the question may not be how much *should* you carry, but how much *can* you carry? Take into account the number of people in your family, their ages, health, normal liquid consumption, and strength. Teenagers, for example, may require more water than other family members. What about the kinds of food in your kit? Have you included food that will require water for preparation? If many of your foods are dried, salty, or spicy, or if they require water for preparation, you will need to pack more water.

If aseptically packaged juices or milk ("soft cans"), or canned water or juices are included in your kit, they will reduce the amount of water you need to carry in the water unit. It also offers variety in taste and nutrition. On the other hand, liquid containers inside a kit use the space that might otherwise be filled with food or other essentials. Prioritize carefully.

Let me repeat: How much you *should* carry is going to realistically be superseded by how much you *can* carry. May I recommend that you fill some jugs or bottles and practice carrying them to your car, down the stairs, to the neighbors across the street. It may seem silly now, but I have had many people report that they just did not realize how heavy a bottle of water could be, nor how it increases in weight the further it's carried.

I strongly recommend that you resolve the water/weight dilemma *now*. One solution might be to have some mode of transporting containers, even a short distance, such as a luggage tote. (See "What if You Have to Walk Out?" in chapter 11.) Water bottles could be attached to belts for easier carrying, although belts made of rope may be uncomfortable. Nylon rope could be used to lash several containers together, creating a handle, or containers could be tied to a polyethylene bucket or backpack. You could also fashion a yoke to wear over your shoulders for carrying water bottles. Or, carry your containers in a school-type backpack if your kit is a hand-carried one.

Water Container Options

Many kinds of containers can be used to carry water. Whatever you use, make sure it is clean, has a tight-fitting lid, and was designed for food or water. The following are a few options:

Canteens and Flasks: Canteens and backpacking flasks usually come with either a strap for carrying, or they can hook onto a belt. Either will work in this situation. One disadvantage is that they only hold a small amount of water.

DON'T BINGE ON WATER

This scene was repeated many times in the aftermath of the Northridge quake. Individuals standing in line at the water trucks related how they had had water stored for just such an emergency. But in the shock and trauma of the situation, they drank up their entire supply within just a few hours.

Commercially bottled Water: Several containers of commercially bottled water could be lashed together to form a water unit with a handle. Or, they could be placed in a sturdy canvas shopping tote for carrying. One advantage of commercially bottled water is that the containers are sealed. There would not be problems of bacteria growth or the necessity of checking and changing the water.

Commercial Water Pouches: Emergency preparedness stores, army-navy stores, and sporting goods stores sell individual four- to eight-ounce pouches of water that could be used in conjunction with a 72-hour kit. One disadvantage is that the containers are neither large nor refillable. Several of these could fit inside your kit, as well as having larger separate water containers.

Water Bottles: Two-, four- or six-quart water bottles with tight fitting lids, such as the Rubbermaid ones found in housewares departments, will work with an evacuation kit. You would have to devise a handle or a way to carry them.

Water Jugs: Sturdy plastic water jugs with a handle, with or without a spigot, are excellent choices to use as a water unit. They usually are two-and-a-half- or five-gallon capacity. A five-gallon jug weighs forty pounds when full. Plan in advance how to transport it.

Picnic or Camping Insulated Jugs: You may already have a two- or five-gallon insulated jug on hand. They work fine. Most have tight-fitting lids and handles. Many have spigots. Keep them full when you're not on a picnic, and they're ready to go.

Plastic Soda Pop Bottles or Juice Bottles: You may have some of these containers on hand. This would allow you to immediately create a "make-do" portable water unit. Use only the heavy-duty plastic containers. Replace them as soon as possible with something sturdier. To use these kinds of containers for water, wash and rinse them thoroughly. If you can smell the former product or soap when the containers are dry, it will affect the taste of the water. Wash and rinse them repeatedly until no smell remains. Lightweight containers such as milk jugs are not recommended—the plastic disintegrates and splits easily. It could leave you with no water when you need it most.

Filling Your Own Containers

Fill the containers until the water overflows. Do not put the lid on if the inside of the container is covered with air bubbles. Gently tap or bounce the container on the counter, causing the bubbles to come to the surface. When the bubbles are gone, gently "top it off," eliminating all the air possible. Then put the lid on securely. This will help reduce the growth of bacteria. Of course, if there is danger that your water will freeze during storage, you will have to allow some space for the water to expand. Otherwise, your containers could break and leak, ruining the contents of your kits.

Note: The water from the tap that you are now filling your containers with is safe. It does not need to be treated or purified. The container needs to be kept as dark and cool as possible, along with the other kit units. Check periodically to see if it has become cloudy or developed any other problems.

Be Able to Carry Water at the Center

Once the water supply is established, you may need a container to carry water from a main source (such as a truck) to your personal or family area. Even if you are relocated into an evacuation shelter such as a large church or National Guard Armory, it may still be necessary to carry water to your area.

If you have chosen containers such as small water bottles or canteens for your lag time water unit, they may not be suitable to carry sufficient amounts of water at this time.

Buckets: A six-gallon-bucket kit container can be transformed

---

IMPORTANCE OF HAVING
A SUITABLE CONTAINER

The importance of having a suitable container in which to carry water was repeatedly reinforced as news broadcasters focused on human struggles during the aftermaths of events such as hurricanes Frances, Ivan, and Jean in Florida and Katrina in Louisiana. Daily, people were shown standing in long lines at the water trucks. Everything imaginable could be seen in their hands, garnered hurriedly to carry water: soda-pop bottles, ice cream buckets, empty bleach bottles, and picnic thermoses.

---

immediately into a water tote. When you pack your kit, tuck in one or two extra-heavy, untreated garbage bags to hold your supplies while using the bucket to carry water while using as a washbasin.

Rubber or Plastic Storage Tubs: If you have used the 10- or 20-gallon rubber or plastic rectangular storage tubs for your kit container, they could be used to carry water. It would probably be more challenging than using a bucket with a handle, but not impossible. Put the lid on, and it will prevent the water from sloshing out as you walk. The tubs also work as washbasins.

Collapsible Water Jugs: Collapsible water jugs with handles and spigots are usually available wherever sporting goods are sold. When empty, they collapse flat to fit inside some kits, or they could be fastened to backpacking frames. They could be tied to a bucket handle or carried inside a canvas tote with the lag time water supply.

Collapsible Buckets: Small, collapsible, canvas backpacking buckets are available in sporting goods departments. They hold about a gallon of water. They are constructed to twist or pop open. A frame supports the walls sufficiently so that a full bucket could be placed on the ground or table.

Purifying Water

The following instructions are included so that if the need arises you would be prepared to cope if only unsafe water is available. If, for whatever reason, the available water is unsafe to drink, you need to have the means of purifying it.

If water is cloudy or polluted, it should be purified before use. If the water is clear but you are not sure whether it is safe or not, purify it anyway. It could contain bacteria, and it is better to be safe than sorry.

You should have the following water purification supplies in your emergency kits:

- A collapsible bucket (if your kits are not in polyethylene buckets) or sturdy plastic bags such as gallon-sized Ziploc bags. (Use only food-grade plastic bags. Colored or treated trash bags will not do, nor will bread sacks or very thin plastic bags.)
- A small pan or large sierra cup in which to boil water.
- Cheesecloth or other cloth for straining impurities from water.
- Heat tabs or other heat source.
- Water purification tablets, tincture of iodine (Although household bleach is usually recommended to use in purifying water, it has been intentionally omitted here because of the difficulty in keeping it or transporting it in a kit container.)

How to Purify Water

If water is especially dirty, strain it through a cloth to remove debris and dirt. Then, boil it at a rolling boil for five minutes to kill bacteria. This is the safest way to purify water. Let the water cool before drinking it. Be sure to take into account the high rate of evaporation at the boiling point and increase the amount you boil. Otherwise, the water could boil away, leaving much less than the amount needed. This may seem like a trivial point, but it could compound the stress and problems of an already-difficult situation. Boiled water will taste better if you pour it from one container to another a few times to put oxygen back into it. This is also true of water that has been stored for some time.

To use water-purification tablets, follow the instructions on the package. Usually, four tablets per gallon are sufficient, or use twelve drops of tincture of iodine. Mix the tablets or iodine thoroughly into the water and let it stand for several minutes. If the water is cloudy, double the number of tablets or drops of iodine. The water will taste better if you let it stand for a little while before drinking it.

Dehydrated Water?

Sufficient water is an absolute necessity. If water could be obtained in tablet form that could be dropped into a container, it would solve many problems. The difficulty is that the label most likely would read, "To reconstitute, just add water." Unfortunately, dehydrated water tablets are not available, therefore another solution must be found.

CHAPTER FIVE

SHELTER, LIGHT, AND A SECURITY BLANKET

When the siren has sounded, it's too late to figure out how you will be sheltered from the stormy elements until help arrives. You must be able to "build" your "home away from home" from the equipment and supplies in your kit. Proper advance planning can provide relative protection and even some comfort. The normalcy created by having a tent to pitch, a lantern to light, and a card game to occupy your mind may not take away all the fear and worry, but it certainly will provide a glimmer of security in the mire of chaos.

As reported in the *Ladies Home Journal,* November 1993, "Apart from financial costs, a disaster takes its toll on victims emotionally, and children are the most likely to be traumatized." For adults the stress is real as well. You possess the ability to lessen at least some of that emotional trauma and stress now by planning, projecting, and providing. Just do it!

Adjust Your Mind-Set—Think Small

The equipment required to shelter you and keep you as warm and dry as desired could easily take up a small room, not just a small evacuation kit. You have to adjust your mind-set to thinking *small, compact, lightweight.* In assembling kits for a family or multimember household, an option to consider is using individualized kits for personal items and filling one large backpack with the equipment that would serve every one, such as a small tent, stove, etc. In order to be prepared as soon as possible, the rule is *always begin with what you have on hand.* Assemble it into a kit, no matter how archaic or cumbersome it may seem. Then, as soon as you can work your plan into your budget, upgrade your equipment. I strongly recommend that you catch the vision of how backpacking equipment can fill a unique niche here. As you read the chapter segments, begin comparisons, and adapt the principles to meet your individual circumstances.

Shelter—Pick up Your House and Go

Probably the best shelter to use at an evacuation area during lag time is a small, lightweight tent. You may choose to remain in your tent rather than take shelter in a community building provided by emergency services. Should you choose to move into the evacuation shelter provided (usually a school, church, or other spacious building), you will probably be in a large room with a concrete or wooden floor, shared by many other people—not a very comfortable or private place. At this point, a small, lightweight tent shifts duties from protecting you from the elements to providing you with some privacy. Of course, this needs to be a freestanding pop tent. I would imagine that you wouldn't find a shelter that encourages anyone to put tent stakes in their floor. Another solution provided by a tent, even if a shelter is in place, is pure shelter. You may end up in a park or football field. Even at a community shelter some people may feel more comfortable in a private tent outside on the grounds where they still have access to the food, water, and bathroom facilities of the center, but without the crowds.

PURPOSE OF A SECURITY BLANKET

During lag time after an earthquake or a severe storm, a small tent might prove to be one of the most desired types of "security blankets" to be found. One firefighter reported that in the aftermath of the Los Angeles quake (Northridge) many people were so frightened that they could not remain inside the shelters or even in homes that were safe. As the ground continued its unrelenting shaking, they persisted in remaining outside—unsheltered.

Check the following options to see if one or more suits your needs. If you have camping equipment on hand, check it out to see whether it should even be considered for an evacuation situation. It may be too old, too large, too heavy, or just too cumbersome to work. It would be more than unfortunate, if you were planning on using your tent, to discover at a critical moment that it won't work.

Tube Tents: Usually constructed of heavy plastic, they are relatively inexpensive and can be purchased wherever sporting goods are sold. They are compact enough to fit inside most kit containers. Normally, they provide very limited space for one or two people. Tube tents could be used for a privacy barrier inside the shelter.

Backpacking Tents: Backpacking tents are usually very compact and lightweight, many weighing only four to five pounds. Many varieties would fit inside a large evacuation kit or backpack, and they are highly recommended for 72-hour kits. They Usually are only large enough for one or two people.

Small Tents: Some small tents work very well as long as you plan a way to carry them. Most would fasten easily to a backpacking frame. They range in size and description, for example, from a two-person, to a two- or three-person pop up round-dome tent.

Regular Tents: If you have tents that you use for camping, you may be able to use them during an evacuation if you have the capability of quickly transporting them, as well as the ability to carry them, if necessary. The obvious disadvantages are the bulk, weight, and size. Most regular tents are much too large for the circumstances.

Tarps or Ground Covers: One or more nylon or plastic tarps or ground covers can be folded flat to fit in or fasten to a kit. If rope is included, a "tent" can be fashioned. It could prove difficult to provide protection from the elements during a storm if the tarp is only large enough to be stretched overhead.

Blankets: a Critical Ingredient

A critical part of your 72-hour kits will be some kind of blanket for each member of your family. Blankets provide warmth and give a feeling of security. A blanket can also be used as a screen to provide some measure of privacy in a crowded evacuation center or area. This is especially important if you have to change clothes or use some kind of makeshift toilet. Blankets become even more important if you live in a locale known for inclement weather.

In order to provide a maximum amount of warmth, I would recommend that every kit contain the combination of a space blanket with another blanket, underneath a poncho.

Use the following list of blanket alternatives to help you determine what you have on hand that will work for now and what to plan to acquire. The major problem with most blankets is how to get them to fit inside a kit. If you are using a backpack frame, wrap it as securely as possible in plastic and carry it as you would a bedroll. If you are using a bucket, for example, after protecting your blanket from water as much as possible, wrap and fasten it securely around the outside of the container. As soon as possible, obtain a blanket that fits inside with all other items as well, to keep the 72-hour kit compact and manageable.

Some Blanket Alternatives

Use the following list of blanket alternatives to help you determine what you have on hand that will work for now and what to plan to acquire. If a description says "bulky," translate that to mean it won't fit in a kit container and still allow room for anything else.

Virgin Acrylic Blankets: Virgin acrylic blankets are warm, have many of the advantages of wool, and yet are lightweight and easily compacted. A twin-sized blanket will fit or squish nicely into a six-gallon bucket with all the other supplies. These blankets also dry quickly. This is probably the best type of blanket for an evacuation kit. Many times lap robes or car blankets found in discount drug or department stores are made of virgin acrylic.

Fleece Throws: You can find fleece throws in just about all stores: discount department stores, drug stores, even grocery stores. The throws are usually smaller than a twin-sized blanket, approximately 50" x 50," and are very affordable. They can easily squish into a kit. Best of all, they dry quickly, yet will keep you warm when wet.

Wool Blankets: Wool blankets are very warm, even when wet. However, they are bulky, weigh a lot, and take a long time to dry. The older 100-percent wool blankets are stiff and nearly impossible to fold. New part-wool blankets would probably work better. Still, they are probably not a good choice.

Thermal Blankets: Thermal blankets are warm but bulky. They dry quickly because of their open weave.

Polyester/Acrylic Blankets: Polyester/acrylic blankets are fairly warm but not as warm as some other blankets. They are also fairly heavy and bulky.

Quilts and Comforters: Quilts and comforters are very warm but weigh a lot, are bulky, and take a long time to dry.

Sleeping Bags: Sleeping bags are very warm, and many are water repellent. If you use a backpack with a frame, you can easily carry a sleeping bag. The bags are bulky, though, and do not dry quickly. The cute sleepover bags designed for children are not in the same category as sturdy camping sleeping bags constructed for warmth. Use them if you have them on hand, but replace them as soon as possible with something warmer.

Down Backpacking Sleeping Bags: Most down backpacking sleeping bags are extremely warm and water repellent and are usually lightweight, though bulky. They do not dry quickly. As part of a kit, they are designed to work with a backpack frame.

Space Blankets: Measuring 56 inches by 84 inches, these "blankets" usually look as if they are made out of aluminum foil. They are very compact, lightweight, and readily available where sporting goods or emergency preparedness supplies are sold. They were developed for the space programs and function by reflecting body heat. Every kit should contain one. They do not have the softness or feel of a real blanket. I recommend that you get the most warmth efficiency by combining a space blanket with a regular blanket or throw. Put the real blanket next to your skin and put the space blanket over it. Every kit should have a space blanket to go with a regular blanket.

Emergency Blankets: A variety of compact and lightweight emergency "blankets" is available. One example is a 5-by-7-foot all-season blanket made of multilayered plastic and aluminum, weighing about 12 ounces. This type of blanket also functions by reflecting body heat. They work well in the kits as a survival blanket, even if used alone. They work best with regular blankets for the greatest heat efficiency.

Disposable Emergency Blankets: They are a compact, lightweight, disposable paper blanket used by medical professionals. They are not recommended for use in a 72-hour kit because they do not hold up under normal use, let alone in inclement weather.

Baby Blankets: Large or crib-sizes baby blankets are warm, though much smaller than regular blankets. They could probably fit inside some kit containers. If used for an adult, they would offer some coverage and warmth. You may want to replace them as soon as possible with a better option.

Blankets Cut in Half or Blanket Material Remnants: You can take advantage of a twin-sized blanket (or blanket material), yet still have a blanket compact enough to fit into a kit, by cutting a larger blanket in half. (The edges can be zigzagged to prevent fraying.) It will still be bulky, but it will only be half as large.

Can You Fit a Campfire in Your Pocket?

It usually is not practical to carry a source just for heat in an evacuation kit. However, if you live in an area known for bad weather, carefully consider the problems of lag time when combined with cold and/or wet weather. Any heat source would have to be small, compact, and lightweight, as well as functional. A practical solution is to use the same source you will be using to cook with. The small folding stoves used for cooking give off some heat. Backpacking and mountain-climbing heat sources are an option. Calculate the weight and volume of fuel needed. Be sure to include matches, disposable lighters, or a fire-lighting device in your kits. Keep in mind that it is unlikely that you will be able to use any equipment that has a flame inside a shelter. But once you are in a shelter situation, you probably wouldn't need a heat source.

Hand and Foot Warmers: Chemical hand and foot warmers do a good job providing heat without the campfire. Squeezing them activates the chemicals, and they will produce heat for about eight to twelve hours. Since they are small enough to fit in your shoe or your pocket, they're a good option for evacuation kits. They are relatively inexpensive, so plan on including several in each kit. Because of their small size, they will tuck in little spaces. They are not reusable.

Shed a Little Light

Every kit should contain a working flashlight *and* some spare batteries. You should provide a source of light for every member of your family. Your flashlights may be your only source of light on a very dark and stormy night. Light is a source of security as well as safety. Think twice before choosing any items that could pose a fire hazard. Advance planning, rules, and safety must be put in place before they're needed. It is particularly important that you hold practice sessions so that the problems of functioning with only your light sources are understood. Following are some lighting options for you to consider.

Caution! The use of any equipment that has an open flame, such as a candle or lantern, requires close adult supervision and safety precautions, especially in chaos! Practice sessions and firm discipline should be mandatory. Be especially cautious in crowded places if children are present.

Flashlights: Standard two-battery flashlights are excellent sources of light. They are safe, and with new batteries and bulb provide about seven hours of light. Heavy-duty batteries and Krypton bulbs last longer. Include an extra set of batteries with each flashlight. The new shake and charge flashlights with LED bulbs may be an even better choice. LED lights burn very brightly and do not need replacement. Check out the options available in size and weight and durability before purchasing any. It may be that a variety will serve you or your family better than just one type. Heavy-duty, waterproof flashlights fill the bill for a 72-hour kit. Larger flashlights provide more light, but have more weight and bulk as well. It is recommended that every kit contain a *working* flashlight (except a baby's or toddler's). Pack it as one of the top items in the kit! If your choice requires batteries, be sure to have new, spare ones in your kit. Even if you choose another light source in your kit, you should still have a flashlight, and it should be packed on the very top. You may need to use it to locate other items in the kit.

Emergency Candles: I mention candles with great hesitation. If you have children, skip the candles and choose a safer light source. Small utility or camping candles may be used in emergency kits. Small "tub candles" designed for emergencies or camping usually come in packages of six and fit in a small candle lantern. "Survival candles" in a can, with one to three wicks, function for both light and cooking. Some have a burning time of 50 hours or more. Long-burning emergency candles, approximately 1½" in diameter, come with metal holders. If you plan on using candles, you would be wise to put them in candle lanterns, which will help support the candles solidly. Small, solid candleholders may be used for the same purpose. Don't choose dinner candles as a light source: they burn too quickly and do not produce a very bright light. The so-called 100-hour candles—a wick in oil that resembles a mini oil lamp—may burn a long time, but they do not produce a very bright light.

Backpacking Lanterns: This lantern is the only recommended liquid fuel lantern for a 72-hour kit. Backpacking lanterns are small and lightweight. Some are collapsible. Consider the weight and bulk of additional fuel. Remember the matches. Safety and caution must also be packed in your kit with the lantern!

Fluorescent Lanterns: Fluorescent lanterns use batteries and usually burn brighter and longer than a regular flashlight, but they are also larger and weigh more. Check out some of the smaller fluorescent backpacking lanterns. Be sure to include extra batteries.

Chemical Light Sticks: A light stick is a plastic tube filled with a chemical substance that glows for a specific time when the tube is quickly bent. Most light sticks are small and lightweight; they last varying amounts of time from 30 minutes up to 12 hours. The light is not extremely bright, and once the stick is "lit," it cannot be turned off. It continues to glow until it is used up. They cannot be used again. Each person would need quite a few of them; they are not recommended as the only source of light for a 72-hour kit. They could, however, be used as a night light for reassurance in a shelter during the night, for children and adults alike.

Clothing: Your Evacuation "Wardrobe"

Past experience with crises indicate that a complete change of clothing, from the skin out, is essential for any three-day kit. The basic purpose for your evacuation "wardrobe" is that in case you become soaked or contaminated in any way during the evacuation/rescue process you will be assured of immediately having clothing to change into. It's not likely that the volunteer

*A complete change of clothing
is essential for any 72-hour kit.*

organizations, with their boxes and racks, will be at the site immediately, and they probably won't be there for several days or weeks.

Even if you do not need your "wardrobe" on arrival at the shelter area, if you have to remain several days, it would be good to have a change of clothing. Research and personal reports indicate that excessive dirt, dust, grime, pollution, and more are basic torments during lag time and the aftermath of disasters.

On a smaller yet just as viable scale, a toxic spill or similar incident could quickly force you out of your home in the middle of the night in pajamas or less. Even for a few hours or one day, it would be nice to have clothing to wear (even without designer labels). Be aware that allergies to wool or other fibers could cause problems if you had to rely solely on volunteer clothing.

You can probably use clothing that you already have on

hand, but you should make sure that it is good, sturdy clothing rather than play clothing, lightweight casual clothing, or worn-out clothing. Don't worry much about designer labels, color coordination, or style. If you can find a few spare crevices in your kits, it would be a good idea to squeeze in extra under-garments or socks, especially for children. The object is to keep your body warm, protected, and dry. Remember that you may be exposed to the elements and to the public, and you will probably be engaged in helping people and in doing hard work. Your clothes will need to withstand the strain.

Depending on your climate, you may want to keep a list of one set of clothing for summer and one for winter and then put the appropriate set into your 72-hour kits when the seasons change. There isn't room in a kit for heavy winter coats, hats, and gloves, but in an evacuation, if your kit is ready, there is usually time to grab them on the way out the door. (Put them on your "don't forget" list.)

The wrong kind of clothing in weather extremes will compound already-severe problems. Having only lightweight, thin summer clothes in the dead of winter would be a serious problem. Heavy wools and sweaters in the middle of a heat wave would be just as miserable. This point must be taken seriously, especially if you are dealing with babies, the elderly, or the ill.

Remember to take into consideration individual needs. For example, support hose are a necessity, not a luxury, for many people. Don't forget such things as neck braces, the scarf that prevents chaffing, dentures, glasses, contact lens requirements, or arch supports.

A pair of sturdy shoes is another critical item. If you do not include a pair in the kit, they must be placed at the top of the "don't forget" list.

Poncho

One item of clothing that should be in every kit is a poncho. Ponchos are generally made of heavy vinyl or plastic and resemble

> *A poncho should be in every kit.*

a cape with a hood. Ponchos are versatile, give protection from the weather, can provide shade on a hot day, and increase your ability to stay warm. A poncho added on top of layered clothing acts as an insulator, trapping warmth underneath it. Practice wearing your ponchos before you actually have to. This is especially important for teenagers, who are so style conscious. Teach them that a poncho is to help them; looking stylish is not a priority here. They are available in adult and children's sizes. Pack ponchos at the top of all kits.

If your container choice is not waterproof, use large Ziploc bags for clothing items. Press out all the air possible.

Clothes for a Baby or Toddler

In providing clothes for a baby or toddler, think large. Six months from now, your child will have grown a great deal. The clothing you include in this kit should account for that. A medium-weight, stretchable, terry cloth playsuit should work well, and it wouldn't matter if it were quite a bit too large. T-shirts and socks are a must! Blanket sleepers might be used instead of a blanket. You can always remove a baby's clothing if it becomes too warm. Put shoes on the "don't forget" list. The kit for a baby or small child will need more consistent

TAILOR THE KIT FOR THE OWNER

I taught a workshop on 72-hour kits for a group of women in a small town in Utah. A good friend of mine belonged to the group. Since she knew I was coming, she decided she had better update her girls' kits before I came. It was a good thing she did. Her seven-year-old's kit contained Huggies and Onesies.

review and updating than any of the others. It may seem like busywork, but it could make such a difference!

Be sure to keep a large package (with handle) of disposable diapers on hand. Cloth diapers will not do because you will have no practical way to wash or store them once they have been used. Don't try to repack diapers into a kit; you need too many, and they are too bulky. Just keep a package next to your kit. Update for size frequently. A good thing to include in a baby's kit is a package of premoistened towelettes.

Because of rapid growth, dietary changes, and other continually changing requirements, a kit for a baby or toddler is one of the most difficult to assemble. Another option would be to methodically create a small child's 72-hour kit on paper. It is essential that you complete this "paper kit" while you have a clear mind and can reason out the items that will be needed. During an evacuation, you could have difficulty remembering such details, particularly if you have more than one small child. If your child has a "security blanket" or favorite teddy bear, be sure to include it on the list. If everyone else's kit is ready, you will probably have time to gather baby's kit following your paper kit. Of course, it would be logical to have a container already prepared with as many basics and spare items as possible. Periodically review and update your paper kit. Make sure you keep it and its container with your other 72-hour kits.

Also, check your child's actual kit frequently to make sure that he has not outgrown the clothing in it and that the other items in the kit will still meet all needs.

If your child cannot exist without a specific pacifier or security blanket, no matter how ragged it is, it is essential to put it on the "don't forget" list. For the toddler, that particular blanket probably ranks in priority with someone else's prescription medicine.

SHORT-TERM SANITATION AND FIRST AID

In the realm of personal preparedness, perhaps two of the most overlooked and underestimated problems during an evacuation are sanitation and hygiene. Since problems usually escalate when you are forced out of your home, these should be planned for in advance.

Once a shelter is set up and functioning it will have rest room facilities, but if water and power supplies are cut off, interrupted, or rationed, you will need to have other arrangements. In some instances, portable chemical toilets may be brought in, but that takes time. During the lag time, you must be able to cope with the situation!

Adequate toilet facilities are especially important during an unsettled shelter situation because stress, a change of diet, lack of privacy, and loss of security compound to upset the digestive system. Good judgment, a sense of humor, and most of all, advance preparation will help solve some of these problems.

Short-Term Sanitation

One important reason to use a polyethylene bucket for at least one of your 72-hour kits is that it can be used as a makeshift toilet. (A collapsible bucket or a backpack just will not work in this instance.) To create a portable potty, you will need the following supplies:

- One or two large, sturdy garbage bags to hold supplies when bucket is used for a dual purpose
- A roll of toilet paper or packets of facial tissue (smashed flat to fit into your kit)
- Some sturdy, extra-heavy-duty trash bags with wire ties (fold them down, press out all the air, roll tightly, and fasten them with the rubber bands so that they will fit in the kit)
- Large rubber bands, at least a quarter-inch wide, large enough in circumference to fit around the top of the bucket, and strong enough to hold heavy plastic bags in place
- Small container of disinfectant (such as the portable toilet chemicals available in recreational vehicle supply stores) to sanitize and help keep odor and germs under control

---

PORTABLE POTTY SOLUTION

At a follow-up session for one of my workshops, a senior citizen returned to relate her solution for a portable potty. Following our class, she had purchased her bucket and then proceeded to the local thrift shop. There she purchased a wooden toilet seat, took it home, sanded and tole painted it. She then securely lashed it to her bucket. She proclaimed, "If I ever have to be evacuated I'll go in style and with class."

- Small bottle of dish detergent or small Ziploc bag of dry cleaner such as Spic and Span, to use in cleaning the bucket when water is available

Insert a garbage sack into the empty bucket with the edge folded down over the top of the bucket. Secure it in place with a large rubber band or duct tape. After using this toilet, put some disinfectant into the bag and cover the bucket with its lid. This toilet can be used several times before replacing the bag. To dispose of the waste, remove the rubber band, twist the bag closed, and secure it tightly with a wire tie. An official at the evacuation center can tell you where to dispose of the bag. *Carry it in the bucket to the disposal site before removing the bag of waste.*

Each member of the family should practice sitting on the makeshift toilet in order to understand balance required, and that you do not sit down hard. It may seem and feel ridiculous. However, it will be far better to feel ridiculous at home now than to compound problems with a personal disaster during an already difficult time. Do not make a seat by cutting a hole in the lid of your bucket. You will need to maintain the bucket with its lid intact as your 72-hour kit container.

If necessary, you can obtain some privacy while using this toilet by having family members or someone hold a blanket in front of it, or suspend a blanket on a rope in front of it. When possible, place the bucket next to a wall or in a corner. This wall will help you maintain balance.

Personal Hygiene Is More than a Bar of Soap

If during an evacuation, you are exposed to mud, sewage, or other forms of pollution, it is a necessity to be able to get clean as soon as possible.

Maintain good hygiene habits in a shelter situation.

Of course, you can survive without a daily bath, but sores and irritation form rapidly without proper hygiene. As much as possible, you should maintain good hygiene while trying to exist during lag time or staying in a shelter. You can brush your teeth, wash your face, comb your hair, and even wash your body with a wet washcloth. This will prevent the spread of disease and irritation, which otherwise would increase the stress during an evacuation. Doing such things as brushing your teeth at a routine time also brings some order to the day, and many times has the healthy and soothing effect of some normalcy. In the past, moms used to say, "Go wash your face and you'll feel better," and that was for everything from a bruised knee to a broken heart. Mom's the psychologist for hard times.

Trial- or travel-sized health and hygiene products are best for 72-hour kits. Some personal hygiene items you might need include the following:

- Bar of soap
- Premoistened towelettes
- Shampoo
- Deodorant
- Toothbrush (travel or camping styles are small and compact)
- Feminine hygiene supplies
- Denture or contact-lens requirements
- Small mirror
- Comb, brush
- Hand lotion
- Lip balm
- Disposable razors, shaving gear
- Baby or toddler needs (diapers, wipes, oil, powder, washcloth, small towel, shampoo)
- Other individual needs

First-Aid or Worst-Aid—You Do Have a Choice

A small and simple first-aid kit should be an integral part of any 72-hour kit. The intent is to be able to treat minor injuries and ailments which could otherwise become serious if ignored for a few days. Be sure that your kit contains a first-aid manual, and read it before you pack it away. Know what supplies are in your first-aid kit and how to use them.

A small, commercial first-aid kit works well. If you would rather create your own kit, contact your pharmacist or the Red Cross for suggestions about what to include in it. As you assemble first-aid supplies—including a commercial unit— keep in mind the problems most likely to occur with you or your family, such as severe allergies. Include the solutions to those situations where possible.

Following are some items to consider for a first-aid kit:
- Aspirin/nonaspirin
- Small scissors
- Antiseptic
- Nail clipper
- Burn ointment
- Tweezers
- Tube of petroleum jelly
- Needle (secured)
- Triple antibiotic ointment
- Antacid
- Cotton balls or swabs
- Allergy tablets
- Adhesive tape
- Matches (for sterilizing)
- Adhesive-strip bandages
- Sunscreen
- Elastic bandages
- Gauze
- Sterile bandages
- Liquid pain reliever, teething ointment, diaper rash, ointment, oil or lotion for baby or toddler

People commonly arrive at an evacuation center without the prescription medicine they must take. If you require prescription or allergy medicine, save yourself future problems by planning ahead now! If at all possible to safely do so, keep a prescription with your kit. Ask your doctor or pharmacist for specific instructions about how to do so. Make sure all medications and their locations are clearly listed on your "don't forget" list!

CHAPTER SEVEN

IMPORTANT
MISCELLANEOUS
ITEMS

During the summer of 1984, a fast-moving, canyon fire forced residents of Malibu, California, to evacuate. According to one newspaper account, a well-known Hollywood personality ran frantically from room to room trying to decide what to take with her. She had only forty-five minutes to decide. Unfortunately, no preparations had been made for such an emergency. First she gathered her valuable paintings into the middle of her living room, but then she remembered other valuables and went to get them. The chaotic sorting and gathering continued, and the forty-five minutes passed too quickly. Finally, she was forced to leave her home without taking anything.

You should decide now, *before a disaster* what you will do with your treasures in case of an emergency. Your neighborhood assessment should help you make plans now about what to do with these things. You may save valuables that would otherwise be lost forever, through panic and indecision. The ability to act quickly and confidently in all of the confusion can make all the difference.

Sometimes the warning to evacuate comes with time attached to the orders. It may be half an hour, or it may be fifteen minutes. If your kits are ready to be loaded into the car, a good portion of that warning time could be spent saving those things that matter the most. Take a good look at your home and decide today what matters most and in what priority. Write it down and tape that list on your kit also. This one thing could definitely make a huge difference for you.

> *Decide today what matters most*
> *and in what priority.*

The Question of Important Documents

Every individual or family has important documents that need to be preserved. These include deeds, wills, insurance policies, birth, marriage, and death certificates, and so on. For many, it is difficult to find a particular document even during normal times. It would be almost impossible to gather up all important papers in an emergency. Also, many people have more than enough important papers to fill an entire emergency kit. There is little semblance of order during an evacuation. In the confusion and possibility of relocation, there is a good chance papers could be lost or inadvertently taken. The possibility of loss or destruction increases with the severity and length of the crisis. A public evacuation shelter or tube tent is obviously not a secure place to keep important documents.

One of the following suggestions, or a combination of several, may provide a solution to protecting your documents. Some of these documents could be required to insure your rights, to prove ownership, and to file claims in case your home is destroyed. Be sure to check your papers regularly to make sure that they are always up to date. The following is a list of documents that you may need to protect:

- Social Security cards and records
- Deeds
- Insurance policies
- Stocks and bonds
- Wills
- Savings and checking accounts numbers and locations
- Credit card numbers and companies
- Passport
- Immunization records
- Family records: birth, marriage, and death certificates
- Inventory of household goods
- Financial records
- Personal and family records, certificates

One of the best ways to protect your important documents is to make several good copies of them. Have these copies notarized, if it will make them more valid in your area. Put the originals in a safe deposit box at your bank. (How close to your home is the bank?) Keep a file of copies at home, as secure as possible. Then give a set of your copies, in a clearly marked, sealed envelope, to a friend or relative who lives outside your area.

Another procedure is to make a list, on one sheet of paper, of all of your policy numbers, agent names and phone numbers—with a short, concise, descriptive note or two. List checking, savings, and credit union account numbers, including names, addresses, and phone numbers of the institution where the account is located. Write down all pertinent names and phone numbers. If the list is extensive, write it on legal-sized or 11-by-17-inch paper; with a computer or at a copy center it can be reduced to fit a smaller sheet of paper. Send one copy to the friend or relative who is out of your area. Laminate a second copy. Slip this waterproof, sturdy copy inside of your kit. It should fit snugly up against the side. Make sure that it can't be read through the side of the container. Heavy tape should secure it in place so that it is purposely not easy to remove.

Another idea is to assemble all documents into one heavy-duty waterproof container, such as a locking metal file box with a handle. Consider it an additional evacuation kit unit. You may be required to "baby-sit" your container in a shelter, keeping a close watch on it to avoid theft. If you are able to use your car to get to the evacuation center, keep it locked in your trunk. Decide beforehand what the alternative plan for your documents unit will be if, in order to evacuate, you must walk out of your neighborhood. Determine whether it would be feasible to carry it with you and what that might entail.

You could also scan a copy of anything valuable and burn it to a CD. Family histories, photographs, vital statistic certificates, anything you are capable of scanning will fit on a CD. This would be small enough to fit in a kit. A copy of the CD could be sent to your contact in another area.

Money

Common sense tells you that even during a crisis, you may need some money for such small things as telephone calls or some gas. Don't forget to take your wallet or purse as you walk out the door. It may be a good idea to include these items on your "don't forget" list, even though in normal times that's usually one of the first things you pick up. (Evacuations are not normal times!) Your checkbook and emergency credit card should allow you to make larger purchases if you need to. One suggestion might be to keep a pack of blank checks and a blank register near the bottom of your kit, along with a ballpoint pen. ATMs won't be working if the power is down, remember?

It would be foolish to try to carry large amounts of money, jewelry, or other valuables with you to an evacuation area. They could easily be lost or disappear. Let common sense be your guide as you keep in mind the size and needs of your family. An unfortunate example of what the cost of simple things could be during a crisis occurred in Los Angeles. During lag time and the aftermath of the Northridge quake, victims were reportedly charged $1 for one cup of water, while the cost of flashlight batteries escalated to an astronomical $12.

You Need a Battery-Powered Radio

A battery-powered radio is an absolute necessity.

A battery-powered radio is a critical kit component. Every adult's emergency kit should include a portable, working, battery-powered radio with an extra set of fresh batteries. *This is an absolute necessity.* Keep the radios near the top of your kits so that they will be readily accessible. Since the duration of an evacuation cannot be determined ahead of time, the spare batteries are mandatory, not optional. After the Loma Prieta earthquake, many people reported that their radios worked for only a short time. They had failed to replace the batteries and had no spares. For family members who think portable radio and CD players are appendages to their bodies, set strict rules on battery usage, or make sure that their kits have an abundance of batteries. However, when the battery power is gone, it's gone, and it's not to be replaced by the emergency supply.

Morale Boosters

In times of trouble, it pays to be prepared to brighten the mood. Discouragement and depression are abundant in the immediate aftermath of serious trouble. There may be hours or days where there is nothing to do but wait. Children are not the only ones to become restless and anxious. Everyone does. The longer the duration, the more difficult the waiting.

If possible, provide the means to boost morale and make

enduring more bearable. If there is room in the kit and weight is not a problem, tuck in small, lightweight items.

A word of caution: Many people are used to playing games on cell phones. During critical crisis time, cell phone usage should be restricted for dealing with the emergency. It could prove to be a lifeline. The cell transmitter may be down or only sporadically functioning. Set usage parameters *before* the situation arises.

You might want to find a way to include some of the following items:

- Small, flat games
- Decks of cards/card games
- Purse/pocket-sized puzzle books, with pencils attached
- Small /pocket-sized books of word games, with pencils attached
- Small pencil sharpener
- Small handheld computer games (with extra batteries)
- Crayons
- Travel-sized games
- Paperback books
- Pencils and a small tablet of paper
- Small sets of scriptures/other small inspirational books
- Small needlework items (include on your "don't forget" list)

However, if space is critical, you can still be prepared with morale boosters. Check out library books that teach simple, fun activities *now*. Prepare a list of these and other old-fashioned family favorites that suit the ages of the individuals you are preparing for. A laminated list of a few concise game reminders and how to play them won't take up much room. It could prove to be a storehouse of nerve-soothing remedies during a stressful time. It will allow you to help others as well. In other words, if physical space is lacking in your kit, prepare yourself mentally.

Don't Forget the Teddy Bear

If at all possible, provide a small and squishable stuffed animal. It does not necessarily have to be for a small child. It represents comfort and security for almost anyone. (I have one in my kit.) A very vivid image remains in my mind. During the lag time and aftermath of the Northridge-Los Angeles quake, the news crews repeatedly showed what appeared to be a college-aged girl. In a daze, she was going through the rubble of what was left of her apartment. She tightly clutched a teddy bear. Several days later, she was in the camera focus again—still clutching that bear.

If your child—or anyone else in the family—has a favorite stuffed animal that they cannot exist without, put it on the "don't forget" list. Again, the setting happens to be the aftermath of the Northridge quake. This time the news crews focused on an anxious mother and a compassionate firefighter going through the rubble of another apartment building. The woman explained that her two-year-old son had not been able to sleep the past several nights without a specific white bear. A few minutes later, the firefighter uncovered the prize— a no-longer-white bear. The mother, with tears in her eyes, said, "He may not have his bed, but he'll be able to sleep now."

A Chocolate Kiss Might Help the Pain Go Away

Being able to have a snack or treat could be just the thing to turn the tide on some otherwise miserable days. Include candy or treats that can double as stress foods, keeping in mind dietary restrictions. Things like wrapped hard candies or sticks of gum might be scattered throughout the kit to fill in tiny spaces, or put in several small Ziploc bags full, remembering to press out all of the air possible. Since quantity potential for treats in the kit is quite small, try to remember to ration it out if you have to use the kit. You may need to issue dire warnings of severe bodily harm if anyone tries to snitch the goodies out of the kits during non-emergency times!

Other Items

You may want to include other items in your kits or, in a family situation, include in a parent's kit. If there is a niche to be found, here are a few items for you to consider:

- Scout knife or pocketknife
- 100 feet of one-eighth-inch nylon rope
- Pocket-sized sewing kit
- Assorted safety pins
- Untreated plastic garbage bags—to be used as a poncho, a ground cloth, or a garbage container
- Duct tape (instead of putting in an entire roll, wrap ten-inch lengths around a pencil or dowel)
- Small scissors
- Small wind-up clock
- Small tools (screwdriver, pliers, hammer)
- Dust mask
- Whistle—to gain attention to get help, not to be used as a toy
- Crowbar—to be kept close by kits but not necessarily in them

CHAPTER EIGHT

GETTING IT TOGETHER, AND KEEPING IT TOGETHER

So you know what the dangers and risks are. You know what you can do about them. You know the different things you need to gather together. It's time to move beyond *knowing* and into *doing*. Getting started is usually the hardest part. But before you head to the cupboard for the flashlight or to the store for the granola bars, get out your pencil and do your homework first. Here's where you figure out exactly what you need to do. It's important to emphasize again: begin with what you have! You can always improve later.

Planning Your Kits

Use a notebook to help you plan what food and equipment to gather or buy for your kits. It will help you plan for your individual needs and get the best prices for what you buy. Keep a record of what you buy so that you don't waste money buying duplicate items. Use this notebook as a reference to help you adjust and update your kits until they are exactly what you need.

Involve the whole family
in the process.

Involve everyone in your family in the planning, purchasing and putting-together process. This will help them to better understand how to cope with an evacuation and to become familiar with the contents of their kit. It also provides teaching moments to discuss how important it is that the materials in the kits must stay there. For example, even though a kit may contain snack items, they are not to be eaten for a snack unless you're in an evacuation situation.

If you can't afford to purchase all of the items now, spread the project of buying supplies over several paydays. Map out a buying system to assure meeting your goal. One suggestion might be to set aside a specific dollar amount each payday to be used to purchase 72-hour kit supplies. I recommend that your foods and "menus" be plotted with a strategy in mind. Begin with "bare bones basics," such as stress foods and compact energy bars. Purchase a variety of these foods rather than spending the whole amount on one food item. Then, systematically add to it, eventually adding in other food groups. This way, should the need arise to use the kit before you have been able to totally stock it, *your* most important "evacuation nutritional needs" are still met.

Purchase any equipment or supplies in the same manner. Your notes and planning pages will help you plot what your priorities are. If you are planning more than one kit, it can sometimes seem overwhelming. Begin with some of the small essentials, such as flashlights and ponchos, or at least one can of canned heat per kit when the ultimate goal is three or four. Work up to a completed kit.

Assembly Tips

In order to make all of the puzzle pieces fit compactly into one relatively small container, you may have to adjust your thinking. The packing will not be accomplished by neat layering. Key words are *cram—squash—push—squish—squeeze* and *stuff.* The goal is to fill every niche, space and spot.

> *Key words are cram, squash, push, squish, squeeze and stuff.*

Take food and other packages apart. For example, granola bars usually are individually wrapped. You can get more into the kit container by putting the bars in individually, here and there, than by leaving them in the bulky square box.

Tightly roll a blanket with the towel and washcloth. Slip several sturdy rubber bands around each end to hold the bundle together. If your kit container is a bucket, place the roll in the center and while holding it, tightly "build" around it. As other items are added, continue to push the blanket down. If a backpack and frame are your kit, roll the towel and washcloth in the bedroll to allow more space in the kit container itself. If the bedroll is waterproof, clothing could be rolled inside of it as well.

What to Pack on Top

To insure your safety and security, there are several items that need to be at the top of each kit; if you are using a backpack as the container, items to be in one specific and easily accessible pocket. They are: a battery powered radio, a flashlight, poncho, essential prescription medications, and a small container with several quarters for emergency phone calls. Also, anything fragile or breakable, such as eyeglasses or contacts, must be kept on the top and protected if possible.

Once They're Assembled, Maintain Them

Do not allow the purpose of your 72-hour kit to be defeated once it is completed. Make it a rule that the supplies in the kit remain intact. Snacking on the foods should be prohibited. Do not "rob" the kit of its batteries or any other items with the promise that you will replace them as soon as possible.

Once assembled, your kits need to be kept in a place as dark, dry, and cool as possible. The number one priority in determining where to keep them is accessibility. The second priority is to protect them from things that can cause rapid deterioration such as humidity, heat, and pests. (We've already discussed snack-seeking humans.)

Keep your kits accessible.

If possible, do not stack them directly on a concrete floor. Concrete "sweats" and promotes the growth of mold and mildew. If your climate is hot and humid, you may want to increase the scheduled checkups outlined below.

Mark Your Calendar—Schedule Checkups

The key is to be aware that once a kit is completed, it cannot be stored and forgotten until a siren wails. Regard maintaining your kits as a rewarding challenge. The alternative could be the loss of time, money, and effort—or worse because of neglect the kit may not function if the need arises. One time we neglected our kits for nearly four years, due to one thing after another, including a cross-country move and a year of serious health problems. I had experimented with adding a second unit to my 72-hour kit that was simply additional food. This bucket originally was filled with pop-top cans of fruit, aseptically packaged drinks, and other ready-to-eat canned foods and packaged meals. The idea is a good one but only if the foods are rotated and replaced every year. After four years of complete neglect, I only had a bucket of rust and slop left. The cans had rusted completely through and the food was spoiled to the point where you could no longer determine what it had been. I had to throw the whole thing away, including the bucket. If I had needed to use my kits for an emergency situation, I would have been in bad shape. Systematically check your kits to make sure they will function when *you* need them. Update and check your entire kit at least twice a year. Mark the calendar. Make it a family activity. A good time to remember to do this is when the time changes and you either have to set the clock forward or back.

Checkup Guidelines

1. Check the entire kit to make sure bugs or mice have not invaded and taken up residency. They invade any and all households, in all climates. A drastic change in weather can drive these pests indoors where you may not have had them before.

2. Check all clothing to make sure it still fits. Growing children require constant clothing updates. Many adults do not remain the same size. Change clothing weight from summer to winter or vice versa. Check clothing for evidence of bugs. Weevil, silverfish, and mealy moths will destroy clothing as well as foods. You'll usually want to wash any clothing, towels, and blankets from the kits. Being stuffed together in a closed container can give everything an odd odor.

3. Check foods to make sure rancidity has not taken its toll. Heat and humidity increase the chances. Check for bugs; tiny pinholes in the packaging or containers or a dust or sand-like substance in the food are an indication of their presence, even if you cannot see them—yet. They can penetrate any container except sealed metal. Adjust baby and toddler kits for

age requirements. Try to adjust for teenager food requirements. (Usually, that means *more!*)

4. Check water containers. If the water is completely clear, it is most likely all right. If there appear to be any problems, change the water in the containers. Refill the containers using proper precautions. Commercial water containers, if still sealed, should be fine.

5. All batteries should be changed at least once a year. If those in the kit still work, transfer them to a household unit for everyday use as they are replaced. Put fresh new batteries and spares in your kits. Keep batteries in their original sealed packaging; they'll last longer and it's safer.

6. If a bedroll or sleeping bag has been kept lashed to a frame, check it for bugs or mice. Unzip it, open it all the way up, and check corners and creases.

7. Evaluate the "don't forget" list. What should be added or deleted?

8. Assess the Important Document List for additions or deletions of policy numbers or pertinent phone numbers.

9. Evaluate all car or office kits for any updating necessary.

10. Mark your calendar now for the next kit checkup.

CHAPTER NINE
EVACUATION
CARE-IN-A-CRISIS

Past events suggest there is a good chance that your neighborhood will someday deal with a major crisis. It only makes sense for neighborhood groups to band together and prepare for it in advance. What is needed is a simple plan, one that can be implemented now, so that survival does not depend on mere chance.

As an answer, Care-in-a-Crisis has been developed. It is a simple, effective means of organizing a network of families, or neighbors, with actions and responsibilities assigned—before the need arises. It is designed to provide the support and extra hands so necessary in a crisis, especially one as frustrating and frightening as an evacuation. Since it may seem during this time as if all is chaos and any control you might have is gone, this is one way to put even a little control back in your corner. Rumor has it that you can't fight Mother Nature. On the other hand, you can at least be prepared to give her a good battle. This is how you can get together with some of your neighbors and put those battle plans in place.

THERE IS NO REASON TO RETURN TO AN EVACUATED AREA

In the spring of 1985, a gas leak in Salt Lake City forced the evacuation of a ten-block area. The late night news was carrying the story live. News cameras were on the scene, and the first thing viewers saw was a woman trying to enter the evacuation area. Police officers held her back as she explained in anguish, "I have to get through! I left my children alone while I went to the store. The oldest is only ten. I must get home!" Calmly yet firmly the policeman told her she could not cross the evacuation line. She had no choice but to turn around.

Evacuation-line Rules

One point that few people fully grasp about evacuations is that once the police or fire department establishes the perimeter of an area to be evacuated, you *cannot* cross that line to go back into the evacuation area. Should your home be in such an area, you *may not* cross back into the area, not even to help your children get out. Once out, you will not be allowed to go back to retrieve a treasure or an evacuation kit. If you don't know where all your family members are, you must still get out. All others have to stay out.

Once the police or fire department establishes the perimeter of an area to be evacuated, you cannot cross that line to go back into the evacuation area.

I think people are confused on this point by the media coverage of the East Coast hurricanes in the last few years. Evacuation orders go out, yet you see stories all the time of the people (including news crews!) who decide to take a chance and ride out the storms in their homes. This is not the same as local police- or fire-department-mandated evacuations. In these, you do not have a choice whether to stay or go. You absolutely must go! Not only is your safety on the line, but also the safety of the police or rescue workers who would have to track you down. In just one instance, for example, a train rolled into a railroad yard in Tennessee with a tank car leaking deadly chlorine gas. Within a matter of hours, the gas had engulfed a surrounding neighborhood and continued to spread. Thousands were evacuated. Some were out of their homes for over five days. Once again, they had no choice as to whether they would leave. To stay would have meant death or serious illness and would have endangered the lives of the rescue workers who would have had to go in later and bring them out.

As for the stubborn people who decide not to evacuate in the face of hurricanes, they do so at their own risk. A friend who endured the 2004 hurricane season (Ivan, Charlie, and Frances) told me that the rescue workers left the last minute they could and still safely get out of the area. My friend's neighbor stayed behind, and he was told to write his name on his forearm with a black permanent marker so they could identify his body when they returned and that he should not expect any help if he was injured because he was on his own until the storm had passed.

> *Evacuation is usually not optional; it is mandatory.*

Evacuation is usually not optional; it is mandatory. Once out, crossing back into a police-declared evacuation area is not allowed. It is therefore especially important that you have your plans in place before a need arises. If you have your neighbors and friends cooperating with you, it will be so much better in all aspects, emotionally and physically.

Have a Meeting—Make a Plan

Who is going to make sure your children get out of the evacuated area if you're not home? Do your neighbors know where you keep your emergency kits? Do they even know you have emergency kits? Is there room in their car to take part of your family as well as their own? The following *Evacuation Topics for Discussion* planning pages will help you work through all the details of how your family (and your neighbors) will be cared for.

Agreeing to be responsible for another person's family in a crisis is a decision not to be taken lightly. If you only have a few minutes to get out, some of those few minutes will have to be used to make certain your assigned family is taken care of. Before you evacuate, you'll need to ascertain whether the parents of the family are at home. If they're not, all of a sudden your job just doubled. In addition to your own family, you must gather any children from your assigned family who are home alone and take them with you. Think through the ramifications of this and figure out how you'll do it. Is your car big enough for two families? Do you have access to two cars and potentially two drivers? I recognize you can never be positive how the future will play out; you may have five other drivers in your family and all or none of them will be home in an emergency. You just work through the possible scenarios as best you can, based on what you have. Perhaps your neighbor would want to leave a key to their car in your safekeeping in case of emergencies. If the parents are gone and a teenaged sibling is watching the children at the time of the evacuation, another driver from your family could possibly drive their family car with their children in it to the evacuation center, if there's not room in one car for all of you. Think it through now.

Be sure to get signed permission statements if needed.

This is one area where Care-in-a-Crisis *disaster* planning differs from Care-in-a-Crisis *evacuation* planning. In disaster planning, you could feasibly watch over several families. In evacuation planning, your helpfulness is limited to the number of people you are physically able to relocate to an evacuation center.

You'll want to discuss with your assigned family the location of their 72-hour emergency kits. You'll need to take them with you during an evacuation if it is at all possible, even if you don't take the family itself. If they are not at home when the evacuation orders are issued, they will still need those supplies when they get to the shelter. You would be the only one who could provide them, since they would not be allowed back into the evacuated area to retrieve them.

If there is time, you will want to lock and care for your assigned family's home the same as you do for your own, including closing and locking doors and windows and turning off heaters or air conditioners. If there is not time, just grab the children who are home alone and the family emergency kits, and shut the door on your way out.

You should leave a note posted in a prominent position (maybe taped to the front door or on the kitchen counter or in a similar highly visible place) stating that you have taken the children with you (or which of the children, if you only have some of them) and where you anticipate going. The parents probably will not see the note until the evacuation orders are lifted, but on the off chance the police or other officers come through the neighborhood, they might be able to pass the word on to worried parents.

---

*Once you take someone's children
to an evacuation center, you must keep
them with you until you can reunite
them with their parents.*

It's very important that once you take someone's family to an evacuation center, or wherever you have to go, that you keep them with you the entire time until you can reunite them with their parents. Both those parents and the children need to know that they can count on you to keep them safe until the crisis is over.

You will want to discuss many issues with your cooperating families. It's a big responsibility to take on the care of another family in a crisis. But on the other hand, it is a big relief to know that someone will be there to help your family if you can't be. The important thing is to make sure you have a plan for your family. Being evacuated will be a frightening, stressful experience. Being apart as a family during this time would be nearly unbearable unless you know you have someone to count on to watch out for them.

Emphasize that no one can afford to take anything for granted. Try to plan for every contingency in specific detail. After plans are in order, calendar regular meetings for updates and revisions, such as every six months.

Be sure to share your decisions with close friends or relatives who do not live in your area so that in an emergency, they will know whom to contact, and they will also not feel that they have to endanger their own lives by coming to rescue you. In addition, keep copies of your plans by your telephone and in your evacuation kits. Also, inform such people as baby-sitters, day-care personnel, and nannies about your plans. It would be a good thing to include the names of your participating families on school records as names of individuals who have permission to pick up your children in an emergency. Most schools will not release children to *anyone* without specific written authorization in their files.

As you make your plans, include neighbors who live alone, have special health problems, or may be physically impaired. Involve them in the planning meetings to evaluate how to meet their needs and to see how they can serve as well.

A Two-Fold Program

The Care-in-a-Crisis program is two-fold. It not only assures others of your help, but you in turn have someone else to count on when disasters strikes. Naturally, you will take care of your own family's needs first. But at the same time, if a program is planned, practical, and practiced, and your own kits are assembled, you will have the time and means to help someone else—even when you are afraid and time is of the essence. To take the program one step further, plan to help your Care-in-a-Crisis families in the evacuation areas.

Evacuation Topics for Discussion

Our assigned family is _____.

Fill out the family information lists that follow with necessary information about this family. Fill one out about your own family for the family you are assigned to.

- What am I expected to do for my assigned family?
- What are their needs? (Are there children, elderly, or handicapped?)
- Are there any special needs I must be aware of (critical medications, asthma inhalers, wheel chairs)?
- Children need to know I have their parents' permission to take them with me in an evacuation situation. Do I have signed permission slips?
- Does my car have sufficient room to transport my family as well as theirs? If not, what other options do we have?
- Where does my assigned family keep their 72-hour evacuation kits? Do I need a key to their home to access their kits if they're not home during an evacuation?
- What is the most likely place I will go in an evacuation (shelter, home of relatives)?
- Does everyone understand the importance of staying together and not wandering off at a shelter?
- What steps will I take to let the parents of the assigned family know that I have their children and 72-hour kits?

Care-in-a-Crisis Plan

Family I am responsible for:

	Name	Address		Phone Number
	Cell phone	Work address	Work phone	General hours
Father				
Mother				
Child's Name				
Child's Name				
Child's Name				
Child's Name				

My specific assignments, during and after an emergency (for this family):

The out-of-area contact for this family:

Name _____ Phone _____ Relationship _____

Care-in-a-Crisis Plan

Family I am responsible for:

	Cell phone	Work address	Work phone	General hours
		Name	Address	Phone Number
Father				
Mother				
Child's Name				
Child's Name				
Child's Name				
Child's Name				
My specific assignments, during and after an emergency (for this family):				
The out-of-area contact for this family:	Name	Phone	Relationship	

Person responsible to help my family:

Name   Address   Relationship

Their specific assignments during and after an emergency:

My other neighborhood assignments:

Tools, skills, and abilities I have that will benefit others in an emergency:

CHAPTER TEN

KNOW THE DIFFERENCE: A WATCH OR A WARNING

"This is a test . . . this is only a test. In case of an actual emergency, instructions would follow on this station. This has been a test of the Emergency Alert System." In case of the actual emergency, you need to know what the warning systems are in your area. During the summer of 1985, a series of terrible, destructive tornadoes struck throughout the Midwest. My husband and I were traveling through this area when the Emergency Alert System broke into the radio broadcast with a tornado warning. As the sky continued to darken, we took shelter in a hotel and watched the television all night as the Emergency Alert System continued to keep us informed about the direction and intensity of the storms. We were advised county-by-county, section-by-section when it would be necessary to take cover and seek refuge. It was a frightening experience, yet comforting at the same time.

The Emergency Alert System

Usually during a crisis, instructions about what to do will come through the broadcast media. Local broadcast stations, especially those with emergency power generators and equipment, provide extensive information about disaster conditions, warnings, what to do to handle specific problems, and how to locate missing family members. They also help restore order and help people to be calm. The standardized Emergency Alert System operates throughout the nation. Your local television and radio networks are tied into the national system.

You Need a Battery-Powered Radio

In a crisis, a battery-powered radio may well be considered a lifeline. Include a portable, working, battery-powered radio with an extra set of fresh batteries in each adult kit. *This is an absolute necessity.* Keep the radios near the top of your kits so that they will be readily accessible. Since the duration of an evacuation cannot be determined ahead of time, spare batteries could be a key to your lifeline. After the Lorna Prieta earthquake, many people reported that their radios worked for

---

NECESSITY OF A BATTERY-POWERED RADIO

The following note was handed to me after a seminar in the Moses Lake, Washington, area. It was six weeks after the Mt. St. Helena eruption. "We all thought the end of the world had come. We never dreamed of anything so ferocious in all of our lives. When the ash hit, we found one thing we never thought of: radio batteries. Not knowing what effect volcanic ash would have on electric transformers, we were told to have on hand a portable radio. We had the radio, but since it had a cord, we never provided batteries for it. Then we couldn't use the radio. We were too frightened to plug it in. We didn't know if the ash would cause an electrical short, or a fire, or what."

---

only a short time. They had failed to replace the batteries and had no spares.

Resist the temptation to just listen to these radios either during the evacuation or prior to. Remember that the main purpose of the radio is to provide information and instructions about an emergency. This might be a good topic to discuss during an evacuation practice session. Discuss it in detail, setting up rules and regulations about how often and how long the radios may be used for entertainment during a lag time or evacuation situation. For those who are truly bonded to their radio or CD player for their existence, a separate category and supply of batteries might just save the day.

Community Warning Systems

In some areas, a community warning system (horns or sirens) will be sounded in an emergency. These are usually tested from time to time, so you probably are already familiar with their sound. If the siren goes off, you should immediately turn on your radio or television for instructions.

If the emergency is a natural disaster, such as a hurricane, flood, or tornado, the radio or television broadcaster may tell you there is a *watch*. That means you will have some time to prepare for possible danger. If the station tells you that there is a *warning*, disaster is imminent! In this case, follow the instructions that are being broadcast, and take shelter *immediately*.

During an emergency warning, do not try to use your telephone to call the authorities to verify that there is an emergency or to obtain more information. Tying up the phone lines might prevent emergency calls from being made. Use the phone only if you have to.

Whatever you do, don't spread rumors. Use common sense. If you hear something that you are uncertain about, verify it before you pass it on. The information you give to others could affect their health, their safety, or even their lives. Sometimes, when rumors are flying, the media will say what information is only rumor.

Other Warnings

Another way you may learn about impending danger is from local authorities such as the police, fire department, or National Guard. Sometimes trained Community Emergency Response Team (CERT) volunteers are sent through neighborhoods. You should follow their instructions explicitly and immediately. This is exactly what occurred in Salt Lake City when a railroad car filled with hazardous liquid developed a leak. As the car sat in the rail yard, plumes of toxic gas blew toward homes nearby. Within twenty minutes, eight thousand people were evacuated.

CHAPTER ELEVEN

GUIDELINES FOR AN EMERGENCY EVACUATION

Practical preparation and carefully thought-out plans, as well as alternate plans, will alleviate much of the confusion and panic associated with orders to evacuate. When you are warned to evacuate your home and move to another location temporarily, there will be specific things to do. I hope by now you realize that it's a lot more than just go out the door, although, as we've seen in some instances, it's a good thing to be able to do.

Maps, Plans, and Practice Sessions

In some instances, you may need to evacuate your home within just a few minutes. You need to know how to get out fast. Part of preparedness should be an escape plan for your home. This consists of a detailed floor plan. Make a separate page for each floor of the home. Using a brightly colored marking pen, show the location of doorways, windows, and stairs. Then, using a different-colored marker, indicate where emergency kits, fire extinguishers, first-aid, and other emergency essentials are located. Clearly show where utility shut-offs are. Mark on the plan the paths to follow in order to get out of each room, the options being doors, halls, or windows. It would be a good idea to laminate this floor plan and securely fasten it where everyone is aware of it, such as on the inside of a centrally located closet door. Place it at an eye level that even the shorter household members are able to see it. If, at this point, you are groaning and thinking, "You've got to be kidding! I need a map of my own home?" Yes, you do, and so do the other members of your household. Remember, the purpose of detailed plans are to help you act calmly, not react blindly, when panic and fear come rushing in as reality bangs on your front door.

Make sure everyone knows how to act and what to do in each kind of emergency. Practice doing the different things. If you live in a two-story home or apartment on an upper floor, practice getting out. In an apartment building, check with the manager and even involve local authorities to schedule on-site help and coordination. Walk through turning off appliances and pointing out utility shut-off locations. This is a critical item on your "to do" list.

Choose and clearly indicate where the family "safe meeting place" is outside of the home. This ideally is not on your property but is still close by—a neighbor's porch or front lawn, for example. That way family members who meet there are out of danger (from problems unique to your own home, at least), but close enough to easily keep track of. For example, for years our family meeting place was our neighbor's front porch. One firm rule was that even though we all loved our neighbors, we all had to remain on the porch until everyone was accounted for. In the dead of winter or in the middle of severe thunderstorms, no matter how uncomfortable or miserable we got, we stayed outside.

Make sure you mark your "safe meeting place" on your escape map. Practice having younger children stay more than just a few minutes in the safe place alone until a parent or a responsible person comes. Involve your neighbors or other responsible individuals. Schedule evacuation drills at least twice a year. These practice drills could prove priceless if the real thing occurs. Research has shown that familiar situations lessen panic. You are more likely to keep your wits about you if you have already practiced what you may sometime be forced to do. Practice sessions will also help you to see where you need to change your plans and make adjustments.

Before a disaster actually comes, practice evacuating both in your automobile and on foot. Focus on the emergencies most likely to occur in your area. If you have not yet taken the time to create your Neighborhood Evaluation planning pages, do so now. The details they reveal could make all the difference in the world to you as you map out an escape route and alternates. For example, a previously unnoticed, dry creek bed, that normally appears harmless, should stand out like a red warning flag after several days of severe thunderstorms, especially if it crosses a road you would consider taking.

Catch a Bus?

Sometimes during an evacuation, buses are provided for those who need them. But lag time can interfere with this, and it may take a while to organize such transportation. As part of your Care-in-a-Crisis plans, organize transportation possibilities with your neighbors as much as possible. If you live in a senior citizen retirement complex, student dorm, or similar facility where the majority of residents rely on outside transportation, find out if any arrangements have been made by the facility's management or by the community for transportation in such an event. If no arrangements are in place, you may need to be the squeaky wheel that gets the oil. Campaign to get an emergency plan in place, and take charge if no one else will. At least, maintain a list of names of those who live in your building or complex, and set up a check-in spot to account for everyone in an emergency (like a "safe-meeting place" for a family, only for your building). This information would be invaluable for police or firefighters. Establish specific meeting places for anyone who would need transportation to an emergency shelter—block by block or every few apartment buildings, for example—in order to expedite the evacuation process. Review these steps in semiannual neighborhood drills.

Do You Have Pets?

If you have pets, take as many precautions as possible to insure their survival. As part of your planning sessions, call the local emergency services or animal control center to see what precautions are necessary and what the relocation center policy is for accepting pets in your particular area. The laws and regulations vary in different places. Sometimes, small pets are allowed if kept contained in pet carriers. In some areas, portable kennels can be set up outside an evacuation center. Animals usually are not allowed inside due to health regulations. If it is permissible and you plan on taking your pet with you, you will need to have a 72-hour pet kit; consisting of food, water, and some plans as to how to take care of animal waste. If water is rationed at the center, you may have problems obtaining any for a pet. However, puddle water, if it is available, would serve for a pet.

Do not simply turn your animals loose, thinking they can fend for themselves. In cases of disasters, such as earthquakes or hurricanes, roving animals may be destroyed in order to prevent more problems and the spread of disease.

Secure Your Home before You Leave

If there is time, *and only if there is time,* and if you have not received other instructions from local authorities, secure your home. Most likely, if you are prepared, you will have time to do so. Two exceptions might be a major house fire or an earthquake.

- Turn down heat/turn off the air conditioner.
- Shut off the gas appliances.
- Disconnect all electrical appliances except the refrigerator and freezer.
- Properly store perishables.
- Lock all windows and doors.
- Park other cars in garages, carports, or driveways; close car windows and lock doors.

Learn how and when to turn off utilities completely. Keep the necessary tools near gas and water shut-off valves. Remember to turn off utilities only if you suspect the lines are damaged or if you are instructed to do so. When the gas is turned off at the main meter into the house, it requires a professional to turn it back on. That can take several days. The National Guard or local police usually patrol evacuated areas in order to prevent looting.

Follow Instructions

Follow the instructions and advice of your local authorities. When you are told to evacuate, do so promptly! If you are instructed to move to a certain location, go there. Don't go anywhere else. In some instances, such as an impending flood or other predictable problem, you may have time to make shelter arrangements in advance with friends or relatives outside of the threatened area. If you have no place to stay, report to the local shelter.

Travel with Care

Usually when evacuated, you leave the area in your own car. This gives you the advantage of continued mobility and allows you to transport your supplies and household members. As a precaution, you should always keep the gas tank half full. Gasoline pumps do not work if the electricity is off, and during a panic you might not be able to get to them. Keep the following things in mind:

In highly congested cities or large urban areas, traffic jams frequently compound problems. Try to maintain a level head and realize that progress may be slow.

Leave as quickly as possible so that you will not be stranded by flooded roads or fallen trees and wires.

As you travel, keep listening to the radio's emergency broadcast system for updated information and instructions. If you drive a small car and are responsible for several people, consider investing in or making a suitable car-top carrier.

If you travel by motorcycle or bicycle, it would be practical to consider racks and/or small utility trailers to convey needed items to a shelter location.

What if You Have to Walk Out?

At one of my workshops, a young, single mother reported that she'd had to walk out of her neighborhood. She said, "They didn't give me any choice, and at the time there was no one to help me. I strapped my littlest girl on my back, put my other child in the front of the stroller, set my makeshift kits on the back of the stroller, and away we went. I admit it wasn't the best, but because I had the stroller we were able to get out." She further explained that because of difficult financial circumstances at the time, the only thing she had been able to use as kit containers were two rather dilapidated quilted diaper bags. And then smiling, she added, "But I tried. I hoped I'd never have to use them, but when the police came and said I had to leave, I could, even though I was so scared."

Under some circumstances, you may be forced to walk out of an evacuation area. For example, there could be a major gas leak and starting cars could create a spark that would trigger an explosion. Or you could be a single car household with someone else having the car at that time. Yet another situation would be that you normally rely on public transportation and for whatever reason it is not functioning. You and your family should plan carefully for such an eventuality, considering the ages, health, and strength of family members; the distance you might have to walk; and the amount of supplies you are planning to carry with you. Almost any type of conveyance will make the journey easier if you have to walk. In some instances having something to work with would mean being able to take at least some supplies with you, or the alternative of it being physically impossible to carry much weight for any distance.

You can carry supplies and children in a wagon, wheelbarrow, sturdy wheeled cart, buggy, or stroller. Several other types of conveyances to consider might be metal marketing baskets (not supermarket carts), sturdy luggage totes, garden carts, and dollies or hand trucks. It would be wise with some of these options to keep rope or bungee cords with them in order to secure 72-hour kit units to them. If there are no other alternatives, and it is necessary to push a person confined in a wheel chair, plan ahead and figure out how to wear a backpack and then attach whatever else will fit to the wheelchair. Remember this discussion is about saving lives, generally in difficult circumstances.

Check in at the Shelter Area

As soon the shelter is set up and begins to function, check in. There will be someone registering individuals and families. It is most important, especially if you have someone else's children with you. It will save officials time as they try to verify who is injured or if there are fatalities. Search and rescue continues until all residents of a neighborhood are accounted for. It will also help the Red Cross, which has volunteers checking for relatives who live out of state and are worried whether their families are disaster victims.

Continue to listen to the emergency broadcast system periodically for advice and instructions. As long as there is any need, updated information will be issued on: (1) where to obtain necessary medical care in the area; (2) where to go for emergency assistance for food, housing, clothing; (3) where to find counseling to help cope with the crisis; and so on.

Returning Home if Damage Is Involved

There are several important safety measures to follow upon returning to a home after an evacuation. Do not attempt to return before those in authority say that it's safe. Shock, personal loss, and anxiety sometimes cloud reasoning and good judgment. Do not visit disaster areas. Your presence could hamper rescue and other emergency operations.

The following safety precautions are adapted from "Disaster Operations," a set of instructions issued by the Civil Defense Preparedness Agency:

1. Use extreme caution in entering or working in buildings that may have been damaged or weakened by a disaster. They could collapse without warning.

2. Don't take lanterns, torches, lighted cigarettes, or any form of open flame into a disaster-damaged building. There may be leaking gas or flammable materials present. Use battery-powered flashlights. Check for leaking gas by smell. Do not use matches or candles. If you smell gas, open all of the windows. Turn off the main gas valve at the meter. Don't turn light switches on or off. This creates a spark, which can ignite gas. Leave the house immediately and notify the gas company or police. Because of the severity of such situations, do not enter the house until an authority tells you it is safe. You have survived so far; don't be careless now.

3. Watch out for and stay away from fallen or damaged electrical wires, which may still be dangerous. Notify the power company or authorities.

4. If any electrical appliances are wet, first turn off the main power switch. Then unplug the wet appliance, dry it out, reconnect it, and then finally turn on the main power switch. Caution! Do not do any of these things if you are wet or standing in water. If fuses blow or breakers trip when the electricity is turned back on, turn the main switch off again and inspect for short circuits in home wiring, appliances, and equipment.

5. Wear shoes at all times until the rubble is cleaned up.

6. Check food and water supplies before using them. Foods that require refrigeration may be spoiled if the power has been off for an extended time. Do not use food that has come in contact with floodwaters.

7. If violence or damage has been involved, check closets and storage shelf areas. Open doors carefully in case there are falling objects.

8. Immediately clean up spilled medicine, cleaning products, and other potentially harmful materials.

9. In dealing with a community disaster, don't drive unless necessary, and then drive with extreme caution.

10. Touch base with the out-of-the-area phone contact, but refrain from tying up the phone lines as long as a crisis condition exists.

Just When You Think It's Over— It May Not Be

Be aware that in severe storms or earthquakes, structural problems and other problems in the home may take several days, sometimes weeks, to rear their heads. Commonly, all it takes is another shake or several more strong gusts of wind to create more havoc where something was severely weakened during the original onslaught. Don't allow complacency to set in. For a while, routinely check things, such as pipes, to make sure all is really well.

It was almost two weeks after the Loma Prieta earthquake. We were trying to return to some form of normalcy while attempting to cope with aftershocks. As my husband left for work one morning, I walked out to the car with him and waved as he left. As I stepped back into the house and passed the 72-hour kits still standing by, I heard a loud roaring, hissing sound. At first I assumed it was from an outside source. I went further into the house and thought I could smell gas. The sound seemed to be getting louder, and now I was sure I smelled gas. I raced to the garage door and threw it open to discover the hot water heater in the corner resembling a scene from a science fiction movie. It was rocking, shaking, and hissing. Clouds of steam were pouring out of it, and the smell of gas was very strong. I yelled and screamed, running through the house, throwing open all the windows and doors. I raced for the phone and called the gas company. The man said they couldn't send anyone out unless it was an emergency because they were still so swamped from the earthquake. (This wasn't an emergency?) I must have sounded desperate as I pleaded with him to stay with me on the phone. I needed to have someone talk me through shutting off the gas on the hot water heater. I found the valves he was describing, but they wouldn't budge. The man said, "Lady, I think you'd better dial 911." I did and waited by the front door with my kits, expecting the garage to go sky high any second. I knew I didn't dare turn my car on to try to get away. The fire department came and turned off the gas, but they couldn't budge the valves either. In fact, they broke off. The hot water heater was replaced, the water and gas restored again. However, the following week the new water heater put more pressure on old pipes already weakened by the quake, and the pipes in the walls burst, flooding bedrooms and the bathroom. Since the aftershocks were still coming, I didn't think the nightmare would ever end.

The clock is ticking. The alarm has already rung. Answer the wake-up call by preparing today for the uncertainties of tomorrow. Organize your evacuation kits now and be ready to survive an emergency evacuation with dignity, confidence, and even some comfort. It's up to you.

INDEX

Index

A

Allergies, 32, 68, 77
Ammunition boxes, 20
Assigned families, 96–97, 99–100

B

Baby or toddler, 33–34, 66, 70–71, 76–77
Backpack, 16–18, 23, 26–28
Balanced meals, 34
Bedroll, 17, 62, 89, 92
Blankets, 62–65